THE NEW DIPLOMATS

JIM GARRISON is Director of the Soviet-American Exchange Program at the Esalen Institute, San Francisco and plays a very active role in promoting citizen diplomacy. He is the author, with Pyare Shivpuri, of *The Russian Threat* and, with Claire Ryle, of *Citizens Diplomacy-A Handbook on Anglo-Soviet Initiatives.*

JOHN-FRANCIS PHIPPS comes from a diplomatic background. He studied psychology at Stanford University, California and is a member of International Philosophers for the Prevention of Nuclear Omnicide (IPPNO). He is the author of *Time and the Bomb* and other works related to the philosophy of peace.

PYARE SHIVPURI is a journalist-lawyer who works out of London promoting positive actions for human understanding and is associated with East-West Reach.

The New Diplomats

Citizens as Ambassadors for Peace

Jim Garrison and John-Francis Phipps
in collaboration with Pyare Shivpuri

GREEN BOOKS

First published in 1989 by
Green Books
Ford House, Hartland
Bideford, Devon EX39 6EE

Typeset in Palatino 10/12pt by
Computype, Exeter.

Printed by Hartnolls, Victoria Square
Bodmin, Cornwall.

British Library Cataloguing in Publication Data
Garrison, Jim, *1951* –
The new diplomats: journey beyond enmity.
1. Disarmament. Human factors
I. Title   II. Phipps, John-Francis   III. Shivpuri, Pyare
327.1′74

ISBN 1-87009-820-X

To our parents,
who have all explored new frontiers of diplomacy

Contents

Acknowledgements

We owe a profound debt of gratitude to Claire Ryle for her invaluable help in co-ordinating our work. Thanks are also due to the following: Professor Christopher Cornford, Brigadier Michael Harbottle, Louise Bolton-King, Catherine Menninger, Thomas Daffern, Polly Howells and Stratford Caldecott.

Introduction

WE HUMANS designed weapons for protection. We graduated from spears and swords to nuclear bombs. These bombs now present us with a paradox. They threaten to destroy what they were meant to protect.

The more we know about the destructive potential of the weapons with which we threaten each other, the more sure we become that our reliance upon them must be curtailed drastically. Both former President Reagan and General Secretary Gorbachev stated that nuclear weapons must be eliminated. And yet the arsenals remain awesome.

Protest against government nuclear policies has been seminal to the public debate. It continues to be important. It is a natural human reaction to the very real possibility of annihilation. Whether or not protest has accomplished an immediate political effect, it has served as a witness to the actions of government. It thereby draws steady public attention to an issue most of us would prefer to ignore.

Disseminating information about the effects of nuclear weapons has also been important. It sets the context for the protest and keeps the public debate well informed.

Those who have protested actively, or communicated factual information about the arms build up, have had to confront a sense of impotence that comes with reacting to a problem without being able to exercise any kind of direct control over its outcome. In this regard, protesters confront the opposite problem of their nuclear-armed governments: their perception of the problem is far greater than their social influence, while the power of their governments is far in excess of their social awareness. Those with more awareness than power feel frustrated. Those with more power than awareness feel irritated.

This state of affairs is leading to a profound split between the problem and the solution, between the exercise of power and the application of wisdom. While the nuclear weapons crisis remains substantially unresolved, our governments are preoccupied with not only maintaining existing arsenals, but with expanding their uninformed power into outer space. The Americans are doing so publicly and officially through the Strategic Defence Initiative (SDI). The Soviets, while decrying 'Star Wars', have a similar substantial programme of their own. Both nations are *de facto* committed to militarizing a frontier that up to this point has been popularly perceived as an arena of peaceful exploration. The militarization of space is being matched by widespread terrorism around the planet itself.

Four decades into the nuclear age, we have succeeded in permeating our lives with violence. Nuclear weapons confront us with violence at the macro level, threatening the earth and humanity's future with annihilation. Terrorism, expected to increase in the 1990s, plagues us with violence at the micro level, threatening our everyday activities with irrational destructiveness. We are now vulnerable at every level of existence, yet we are being swept into developing ever new forms of violence, even on our roadway to the stars.

This violence is generated by our failure in creative diplomacy. Instead of seeing neighbours around the world linked by mutual interests, we persist in seeing enemies separated by conflicting ideologies. In the west, the support for our massive arsenals is intertwined with our perception of the 'Soviet threat'. The Soviets justify their equally lethal arsenal by their perceptions of the 'American threat'. Accepting the notion of 'the enemy' and relying on violence are two sides of the same coin.

To a large degree the public on both sides either actively or numbly accepts this state of affairs. Yet a growing number of people are looking for ways to break out of a spiral that can end only in mutual destruction. The increasing recognition that our support of weapons of mass destruction is linked to our perceiving other human beings as 'enemies' is creating a new diplomacy. Like public protest and the dissemination of information about nuclear weapons, the new diplomacy is coming not from the governments that wield power, but from the people who want to spread awareness.

The nuclear age is generating citizen diplomats who are insisting that since nuclear strategy is linked to territorial factors and perceptions of 'the enemy', we need to look into both with equal acuity. Across the political spectrum people are recognizing the need to balance the negative emotions associated with nuclear weapons with positive activity concerning fellow human beings. Having become increasingly aware of the medical and biological consequences of a nuclear exchange, many are now rethinking their relationship to the people against whom their governments hold weapons.

In this vulnerable new world, citizen diplomacy is challenging us to reconnect with those from whom our governments, our fears and our arsenals have divided us. To do this, we need to understand how we create enemies, how we reinforce negative perceptions of one another and how we can transform our perceptions so that enemies can become neighbours.

The impulse for citizen diplomacy is coming largely from the US, the first nation to drop the Bomb and the nation with the largest nuclear arsenal. In Europe, a potential battlefield, other types of diplomacy are emerging. The Greens of West Germany have opened up possibilities in parliamentary democracy with their development of the politics of 'deep ecology'. Solidarity in Poland has broken down the psychological dominance of Soviet and communist control in eastern Europe.

All three of these movements have brought together visions of human potential with an awareness of the reality of political limitations. In the face of the great divisions between east and west, American citizen diplomats are developing and sustaining innovative contacts based on equality. In the frontline state of Germany, crowded with nuclear weapons and foreign troops, the

Greens are developing the politics of interconnectedness and environmental concern. In the midst of a totalitarian nation bordering the Soviet Union, Solidarity has engaged in a 'self-limiting' revolution which has made the process of revolution as important as the goal of freedom.

If nuclear weapons are based on the politics of exclusivity, these new types of diplomacy are based on the politics of inclusivity. If nuclear weapons are predicated on the attempt to gain limitless power, these new kinds of diplomacy are predicated on the pursuit of the wisdom of limits.

The facts provided by physicians and scientists about the effects of nuclear war are easily and widely available, yet public understanding about the psychological processes involved in the formation of enemy images has barely begun. This is not because studies do not exist, but because little attention has been paid to this aspect of the situation.

We write in the conviction that our understanding of enemy-image formation, coupled with what is already known about nuclear weapons, could release an enormous amount of energy –currently directed against 'the enemy' – for forging a neighbourly relationship.

Our aim is also to describe the psychological basis and the underlying principles of the new diplomacy that the citizen diplomats, the Greens and Solidarity represent, showing that despite the vastly different contexts in which they have arisen and operate, they are partaking in a common vision of the future of humanity – a vision that is based on the empowerment of the individual to help decide the destiny of history, the belief in openness, truth and trust as the cornerstone of human relation-ships and the conviction that, in political conduct, means are as important as ends.

The 'new thinking' of Mikhail Gorbachev in the Soviet Union is offering unique opportunities for creative response from the western side. Gorbachev is depriving the west of an enemy. He is democratizing the Soviet political structure, implementing free market principles in the economy and offering dramatic reductions in nuclear weapons. He is clearly a world-class statesman with a vision of a different future for humanity.

Nevertheless it would be a mistake to think that several decades of negative cold war psychology can be instantly dissolved by Gorbachev's policies of *glasnost* and *perestroika,* or a series of summits, or negotiated treaties. These changes are real enough and point in the right direction, but the hostility and mistrust run deep. It will take time for the new diplomacy to take hold.

Glasnost and *détente* can only work if we, the people, want them to work. Peace is not made between leaders; it is between peoples.

Jim Garrison
John-Francis Phipps
Pyare Shivpuri
London, 1988

---- 1 ----

The cold war insight gap

'I DON'T know what came over me,' are the familiar words of an apparently rational person looking back with wonder and remorse on his or her sudden explosion of wrath. They might also serve as the collective expression of a nation, for example the Germans looking back on the Nazi era. Humanity is now faced with forms of destruction on an unprecedented scale. The degree of insight now required of us is equally unprecedented. Hitherto the Socratic injunction 'know thyself' has been generally regarded as an optional extra, reserved only for an elitist group of illuminati. But what was previously perceived as an elitist option has now become a psychological imperative for each one of us.

Over the past three decades, many competent studies have been undertaken into the psychological aspects of war and conflict resolution in the nuclear age without any appreciable effect on actual policy making. Indeed, it is almost as if such studies did not exist. What we know about ourselves and the manner in which government officials conduct international affairs on our behalf are divided by a vast 'insight gap'.

It is all too easy to be seduced by the illusion that because we live in a modern, technologically sophisticated world, our psychology, our attitudes and our ways of thinking all correspond neatly with our times. The former Astronomer Royal, Sir Martin Ryle, remarked shortly before he died in 1984 that 'our cleverness has grown prodigiously - but not our wisdom'. Yet even as we nod complacently at this, we tend to stop short of actually promoting the growth of wisdom in ourselves. One of the greatest fallacies of our age is the assumption that human problems can be solved by cleverness alone.

When relationships go wrong, we know how easy it is to project all our own shortcomings, fears and frustrations onto the other party. We may also have had the unpleasant experience of being on the receiving end of a demon image. In such a situation everything we do, even if done with sincerity and with the best of intentions, is misperceived.

We may also know about self-fulfilling prophecies: in focusing exclusively on negative aspects of a person's character, we are in reality setting things up to ensure that the person in question will exhibit only those negative attributes, thus confirming our pre-existing image.

The cold war is predicated on such projections and self-fulfilling prophecies. It has also become a societal addiction. Our strategists plan for it; our scientists design the weapons for it; our corporations profit from it; our armed forces prosper on it; our politicians rationalize it.

The vast military-industrial-scientific complex that initially arose because of the cold war now generates it. It has become a self-perpetuating enterprise of gargantuan proportions. Neither the cold war nor the military-industrial complex serve our true interests; instead, whether passively or reluctantly, we now serve it, interlocked into perpetual conflict, both psychological and material.

Referring to those who perpetuate this enterprise, Harold York, first Director of Defence Research and Engineering at the United States Department of Defence, argued that 'the guilty men and organizations are to be found at all levels of government and in all segments of society; presidents, presidential candidates, governors and mayors, members of Congress, civilian officials and military officers, business executives and teachers, famous scientists and run-of-the-mill engineers, writers and editorialists, and just plain folks'. These people are not disembodied cold-warrior phantoms: they are ordinary individuals who go out to work in the morning, come home in the evening, watch television, kiss their children goodnight and feed their pets. Yet while individually quite normal and sane, they collectively co-operate to devilize other social groups and build weapons through which they seek to protect with the threat of extinction the things they value.

We now take the cold war so much for granted that it seems part of the very air we breathe. Persistently threatening other nations with nuclear annihilation seems to have become a permanent part of the 'fixtures and fittings' of the political aspect of our life. Even though our commonsense tells us that all parts of the world are inhabited by human beings very much like ourselves, with similar hopes and fears, despite cultural and ideological differences, our primary political perception is in terms of the east-west divide. The primacy of our common humanity has been relegated to second place. Somewhere in the process our perception of shared humanity has been distorted, if not altogether eclipsed.

The very term 'cold war' seems suitably abstract, something remote for which 'they' are responsible, not us. But the cold war is by no means as remote as we would like to think. Nor is our collective refusal to demand and apply insight merely an abstraction. We are all caught up in it to varying degrees. In this way, the cold war involves us all in a continual dehumanizing process which, paradoxically, includes ourselves.

From the psychological point of view, the west has been at war with the Soviet Union since the Bolshevik Revolution of 1917. And just as the concept of the 'Red Menace' has been deeply instilled into the collective western psyche, so hatred for 'western imperialism' has been as deeply embedded in the Soviet psyche. Consequently, our perception of each other is primarily military-strategic and predominantly hostile.

Yet it is not war that is at issue here, not even a 'war to end all wars'. Since Hiroshima, we can only talk realistically of omnicide – a term coined back in the 1940s by the American philosopher, John Somerville, to bring out the fact that the use of nuclear weapons involves the death of all. If we bear this in mind, he wrote, 'there will be less temptation to argue that we might win omnicide, or survive omnicide, or profit from omnicide, or wage a just omnicide'.

It is a well known phenomenon in counselling work and therapy, especially when any kind of addiction is involved, that patients can only begin the journey towards integration when they acknowledge the fact that they have 'touched bottom'. The trouble arises when the addicts try to kid themselves that this personal hell is a normal state of affairs. If recovery is to take place, the addiction has to be recognised for what it is: abnormal and dehumanizing. The same principle applies to our international addiction to the cold war and the omnicide it implies.

Just as the drug addict or the alcoholic has to take the first step by really wanting to break the habit, so the cold-war addiction can be brought to an end only if enough of us really allow ourselves to see that as nations we have 'touched bottom', and as citizens we are condoning an addiction being waged on our behalf.

The growth of wisdom – which, in this case, is simply another name for psychological insight – always entails an initial phase of strong resistance, since it involves stopping games of self-deception and facing up to some painful realities about ourselves personally and our societies collectively. It also involves looking the nuclear threat in the face and not averting our gaze from its horror.

We need to understand that our nuclear weapons are not only the cause of the present crisis, but also its effect. It is a fundamental psychological fact of life that the repression of unpalatable truths about ourselves personally or our societies collectively tends to fester away in our unconscious, building up proportionately greater destructive energies. The greater the repression, the more powerful the eventual explosion of irrational forces. Just as an individual who may appear to the outside world to be perfectly sane may suddenly explode in a fit of irrational fury, so a whole nation, previously perceived by the world at large as being reasonably civilized and tolerant, may find itself carried away on a tide of jingoistic hysteria and state-sanctioned mob violence.

Carl Jung pointed out that each one of us has a negative or dark side in our psyches which contains all our weaknesses, insecurities and destructive tendencies. No matter how much we like to deny the 'shadow', it is a natural and necessary part of our psychological reality. Whenever we project our own darker side onto some

4

other person or group, we are in fact depriving ourselves not only of something that is our own, but which is also necessary for our own growth. Moreover, we only project onto others that which we lack the courage to confront in ourselves. We tend to see our dark side as something weak, something evil, something shunned. In understanding the weakness of the 'shadow' on the one hand and its importance in completing our personality on the other, we realise new sources of creative energy. One has only to imagine the benign effects of such insight applied on a socially significant scale and how this could transform the conduct of international relations.

Similarly, if the feminine element in our psyche is denied or repressed, the unbalanced masculine element tends to become externalized in an exaggerated ultra-macho form. No war could ever be fought without this isolating process. The pseudo-psychology of the cold war is equally dependent on this same repression. If the masculine-feminine balance in the psyche is achieved on a socially significant scale, popular pressure for a radical change in the conduct of international affairs would be irresistible. Possibly the most dangerous and certainly the most widespread myth of the nuclear age is the idea that facing this reality will drive us mad, while denying it will somehow keep us sane. The reverse is in fact the case: madness does not lie in facing the truth, it lies in denying it.

The psychiatrist Dorothy Rowe asked some of her professional colleagues how they managed to live with the nuclear threat. She found that several, especially those in the middle of their careers, attempted to deny the problem completely and expressed surprise that she could even ask such a question. It was, Rowe comments, 'curious to hear people, whose job involves deciding whether another person is mad, advocating what we regard as the measure of madness' – that is, being out of touch with reality.[1]

One of the most common forms of denial is the defence mechanism known as displacement. It entails what the word literally means: the actual underlying fear (which is too dreadful to contemplate) is displaced onto other anxieties, concerns and obsessions. When we look at the way our own society is structured, we find that its design induces virtually continuous displacement.

Our economic anxieties are predominant over nuclear anxieties. Most of us are more worried about rent or mortgage payments. Even in the 'nuclear' family, both parents now commonly go out to work. They come home tired and sometimes depleted and many are not able to even enjoy their children, or one another. The last thing they want, on top of all this, is a major social problem to contend with. If they do galvanize themselves to attend a local meeting on broader global issues, they are unlikely to confront the prospect of possible planetary destruction with the kind of charged activity it deserves.

Joanna Macy, who has played a leading role in setting up groups specifically designed to address nuclear reality, writes:

> Seeking escape from the 'unthinkable', our society turns increasingly to a desperate pursuit of pleasure and short-term goals. The 'new hedonism' evident in the consumption of goods, sex and entertainment – and the cult of pursuit of money as an end in itself – are so striking today as to suggest that they derive from more than sheer appetite. The frantic quality to it all does not convey a healthy lust for life so much as the contrary; and it suggests a profound doubt in the goodness of life and a sense of impending loss.[2]

One thing is certain: clearer perception of our own epoch cannot come about by denial, psychic numbing, repression, projection and displacement of our nuclear *angst* onto other lesser concerns. Somehow we have to work through the darkness and penetrate beyond the 'despair barrier' – not towards a facile, naive optimism but towards a more genuine understanding and acceptance of our reality and a more life-affirming philosophy.

The literary critic Philip Toynbee, who suffered much personal anguish from depression, came to the conclusion that depression itself is often a sign, a signal from the unconscious, that some kind of profound inner change is called for. Similarly, our collective nuclear *angst* may also be a signal from the deeper regions of the western psyche that we too must undergo an inner change of historically unprecedented proportions.

Hiroshima may prove to have been the death knell of the human race. Hiroshima could also be a signpost to a new world order. Our capacity to undo Creation could compel us to take the road of wisdom, living with our disappointments in one another and limiting voluntarily our power over each other. The activities of the protestors, the information gatherers, the citizen diplomats, the Greens, Solidarity and the Gorbachev revolution all indicate that in the midst of militarism and cynicism, human renewal is taking place. Which option will prevail is at present an open question, although perhaps we can look with more than hope to the words of the poet Theodore Roethke: 'In a dark time, the eye begins to see.'

—— 2 ——

Absolute weapons, absolute enemies

IT MUST be one of the supreme ironies of modern history that Americans and Russians fought together against the Nazis during the Second World War and then equated each other with the Nazis after the war. Barely was the Armistice signed in 1945, when George Kennan, then US ambassador to Moscow, dispatched his famous 'long telegram' to Washington, reminding the US State Department about the 'inherent' tendency of the Soviet Union to expand. In 1950 the National Security Council document NSC–68, a top secret report on Soviet intentions, warned that:

> The Kremlin's policy towards areas not under its control is the elimination of resistance to its will and the extension of its influence and control. It is driven to follow this policy because it cannot . . . tolerate the existence of free societies; to the Kremlin the most mild and inoffensive free society is an affront, a challenge and a subversive influence. Given the nature of the Kremlin, and the evidence at hand, it seems clear that the ends towards which this policy is directed are the same as those where its control is already established.[1]

The author of NSC–68 stated that the USSR could never act like Britain, France, Germany or the US, who by choice would be willing to share areas of influence. NSC–68 asserted it was in the very core of the Soviet character to expand. The model NSC–68 used to analyse Soviet intentions was that of Nazi Germany. The fact that the Soviet Union had a completely different social structure in an entirely different historical context was ignored. Although NSC-68 was never officially adopted by the Truman administration, it was generally viewed as a turning point in US and western European assessments of Soviet intentions and behaviour. Its effect was to cause two transformations of perception. First, it called for major increases in defence spending to counter the Soviet threat; and second, to quote former Secretary of State Dean Acheson, it was used 'to bludgeon the mass mind of "top government" so that not only could the President make a decision but the decision could be carried out'.[2]

After NSC-68, dissenters had a very difficult time getting a hearing. Now more united and in possession of an authoritative document to use for bludgeoning, the governing elite could convey the impression of the Soviet threat with greater clarity to the public of America and western Europe. In this way they could obtain support for the particular foreign policy programmes they wanted to put in place: initiatives that would 'contain' communism.

During times when the governments of either the US or NATO countries felt it necessary to remind their peoples just how bad the Russians really are, other such documents appeared, reiterating the same basic themes. The best-selling books of Henry Kissinger and General Maxwell Taylor during the 1950s prophesied US and NATO weakness in the face of the Soviet threat. In 1957, the Gaither Report warned that the US and NATO were actually falling behind the Soviets and the Warsaw Treaty Organization (WTO). Reaffirming the NSC-68 consensus, the Gaither Report made one point in particular which has haunted US and NATO policymakers ever since: that soon the Soviets would have enough ICBMs to overwhelm NATO and American defences. The Gaither Report urged, in the strongest possible terms, higher defence budgets and the immediate indoctrination of the public to the dangers at hand.

In 1976 a group calling itself the Committee on the Present Danger was founded in the US. It was composed of high-ranking conservative politicians, military specialists and foreign policy experts. Warning that a new wave of Soviet expansionism was beginning, its report stated: 'The principal threat to our nation, to world peace, and to the cause of human freedom is the Soviet drive for dominance . . . The Soviet Union has not altered its long-held goal of a world dominated by a single centre – Moscow.[3]

Since 1945 the US and its NATO allies have been gripped by a 'Munich complex'. In 1938, Chamberlain had declared 'we will have peace in our time', after a meeting with Hitler in Munich, during which he had acquiesced to Hitler's demand to take over Czechoslovakia in return for a promise by Hitler to stop his foreign expansionism. The west has been haunted by this appeasement ever since, fearing that any acquiescence to Soviet expansionism could end in either world war or, worse, Soviet takeover.

Since 1917, the Bolshevik government has used the threat of 'imperialist encirclement' to bludgeon the mass mind of the Soviet people. The result has been that the 'American threat' has become as real to the Soviets as the 'Soviet threat' to the Americans. Soviet policymakers have also been preoccupied with the lessons of the Second World War. This has meant primarily an obsession with the fear of invasion. Almost to the same degree that the US has been encumbered by a 'Munich complex', Soviet post-war thinking has been influenced by a 'Barbarossa complex', the code name of the German surprise attack in June 1941. In their struggle against the Nazis, 20 million Soviets lost their lives and most of the Soviet Union west of the Urals was devastated. The result of this experience has been the Soviet missile build-up in the early 1960s and the call for the Soviet people to be in a state of 'constant readiness'. 'We do not want to find ourselves in the position in which we were in 1941,' states Soviet Marshal Malinovski, 'This time we shall not allow the imperialists to catch us unawares.'[4]

With China to the east rapidly gaining the capacity to target most of the important Soviet cities, the Soviets are doubly concerned about defending themselves from a nuclear attack. They are alarmed by both the US notion of 'limited' nuclear war, in which 'selective targeting' and 'counterforce' attacks could occur, and by the US determination to proceed with SDI, the so-called 'Star Wars' programme. Even in the 1980s, still not having recovered fully from the enormous losses they suffered in the 1940s, the Soviets are determined never again to be 'surprised'.

Gorbachev has not altered this basic doctrine, although he has developed what has been termed 'asymmetric response'. While the Soviet Union will keep up, it will no longer concern itself with parity in bombs, bombers, missiles and warheads. Gorbachev has decided that, having achieved parity, the Soviet Union can act, rather than react to the United States.

It has been said that two types of countries are the most paranoid: the ones that have never been attacked and the ones that have constantly had to repel attack. The only time the United States mainland has ever been attacked was in 1812 by the British. Practically speaking, Americans simply have no experience of war on their territory. Foreign armies have not marched on American soil; only foreign immigrants have. Wars have always been something they have fought elsewhere. Even their first loss, in Indo-China, was experienced through public protest and media exposure.

The Soviets have been invaded repeatedly since the Mongols conquered Russia in the thirteenth century. They have also invaded neighbouring countries, and because of this the Soviet Union now constitutes the largest land empire in recorded history, containing over 100 nationalities. Afghanistan has been only their latest attempt to extend their control and is the first failure of the Red Army. Having been invaded twice by western Europeans – by Napoleon in 1814 and Hitler in 1941 – the Soviets now hold eastern Europe as a *cordon sanitaire*. They have become masters at using the threat of invasion not only to legitimize domestic repression but to sanction foreign expansions.

It was the British physicist and naval officer P.M.S. Blackett who first stated that people could tolerate immense nuclear stockpiles only if they were convinced that those weapons protected them from a truly demonic opponent. 'Once a nation bases its security on an absolute weapon, such as the atom bomb', he said, 'it becomes psychologically necessary to believe in an absolute enemy'.[5] The German physicist Max Born seized on this idea, saying, 'to quiet the consciences of human beings concerning military plans which conceive of the killing of tens or hundreds of millions of men, women and children on the other side – and on one's own side, which is not even mentioned – the other side must

11

be viewed as essentially corrupt and aggressive'.[6] Blackett and Born spoke these words in the 1950s. Time has proved them to be true.

Absolute weapons require an absolute enemy. A policy of omnicide requires and demands a totally demonized and dehumanized perception of the assumed adversary. Cold-war doctrine entails something more concrete than ideological confrontation. It requires government of the bunker, by the bunker, for the bunker.

This denial of life is rooted in a radical doubt of the values we claim so ardently to be defending. As Thomas Merton wrote in 1965:

> If our civilization is what we say it is, if our values are as high as we claim them to be, then our society ought to be possessed of a vitality, a sanity, a creativity, a resourcefulness that would enable us to survive any economic or political crisis, while the communists would inevitably collapse under the weight of their own inconsistencies and leave us in peace . . .
>
> While claiming to believe in democratic ideals and freedom, the western way of life admits in reality a radical doubt of all those values. It has no practical faith in them because it cannot believe they have retained enough power to overcome communism. Only nuclear weapons can do the trick. This attitude . . . springs from the emptiness, the resentment, the sense of futility, the meaninglessness which gnaw secretly at the heart of western man.[7]

The Soviet government has its own fears, self-doubts and insecurities, in particular over its ability to hold together fifteen republics comprising over 100 different cultural groups. But there is also a deeper self-doubt, of a more philosophical kind, about whether its own Marxism-Leninism can continue to actually work. Gorbachev is admitting in effect that as constituted, it cannot. The question is what the success of his reforms will mean for the Soviet empire.

The supreme irony of it all is that by virtue of this melancholy dynamic, we in the west contribute to the very repression we are so quick to condemn in the east, while official Soviet propaganda contributes directly to the very profits from US research and development in defence which the Soviets are so quick to condemn as the ugly face of capitalist imperialism. In many ways the cold war is conflict by consent.

Believing in a philosophical iron curtain, a rigid Berlin wall separating one causality from the other, suits the west as much as it suits the east. Each side would like to perceive causality as working in a neat, clear-cut way. In the west, we perceive independent Soviet peace groups being persecuted by state authorities. It seems a straight causal connection: dissidents speak out and the KGB oppresses them, therefore the Soviet empire is evil and we in the west must keep up our nuclear shield, be strong in the face of the Soviet threat, negotiate from strength, and so on.

In the east, the Soviets witness the wealth of the industrial democracies of western Europe, North America and the global reach of the multinational corporations. Therefore, they conclude, these nations are gripped by monopoly capitalism and the inevitability of war, and the Soviets, having been attacked before, must keep parity with all American military advancements.

Even when the Soviets offer to lessen the tensions, as Gorbachev has done, there is the underlying suspicion that he is trying to catch us off balance and take advantage of us while we are vulnerable. No less a figure than Henry Kissinger has warned the NATO alliance that a reformed Soviet Union would be a more dangerous adversary.

Both superpowers suffer from the same distorted perceptions. Because deterrence resides not in the weapons, but in the minds of those who order their creation, hostility against 'the enemy' has to keep abreast of the governments' military postures. Otherwise the very concept of deterrence itself is endangered and, according to this kind of thinking, so is peace. If either side were to relax its determination to set the apocalypse in motion, it could trigger the aggressive designs of 'the enemy' who is poised and waiting for 'our' resolve to weaken. The poignant paradox of the socio-political situation in which we live is that our governments are telling us that our peace is threatened by the outbreak of a peace-loving attitude. We are told that our peace cannot endure trust; that only suspicion, mistrust, hatred and fear can guarantee our security.

The emotional responses needed to sustain the policy of deterrence were hardened long ago. Most of us are not even aware of their basis. The hatred and suspicion have been processed into abstract concepts and technical language. Any doubts are not about the wisdom of the deterrence but the intentions of the enemy. The result is that world peace has come to mean the absence of war directly between the superpowers. The fact that since 1945 there have been over a hundred armed conflicts all over the globe is considered of little consequence. Instead of looking at our own motives, we look at the capabilities of our weapons. They rather than we have become the primary actors on the international chessboard.

The speed of rockets, the efficiency of deployment schedules, the accuracy of warheads and first-strike capabilities have become the indicators of how we 'maintain the peace'. The moral or political will of the people functioning behind these weapons has become redundant. As a result, military technocrats dominate the discussions of arms control and the question of peace is no longer how we can live together in mutual tolerance, but how we will work out the data sheet so that the mutual balance of terror will hover at a stalemate.

The ritual format of the nuclear debate demands that we be 'reasonable' and limit our discussion to the numbers count. Yet while the motives of hatred and mistrust are treated as irrelevant side effects of objective events, they are built into the official intelligence analyses on which 'threat assessments' depend and upon which nuclear weapons decisions rest. No wonder, then, that so few citizens have persisted in understanding that before substantial reduction in the number of weapons can be achieved, denial, paranoia, persecution complex and fear must be eradicated and trust building begin.

Einstein was one of the first to realize the solution to the problem he had helped to engender. He said: 'Everyone sees that under the present conditions a serious military conflict (in fact, even the preparation for a possible military conflict) must lead to the annihilation of all mankind; nevertheless, men are unable to replace cunning and mutual threats with benevolent understanding.'[8] The only way out of this predicament, he observed, was to realize that 'the precondition for a real solution of the security problem is a certain mutual trust by both parties, a trust which cannot be replaced by any kind of technological measures'.

—— 3 ——

Enemy images

IN AN article that appeared in 1960, aptly entitled 'Breaking the Thought Barrier', the psychiatrist, Jerome D. Frank, explored some of the processes involved in the formation of enemy images. Frank pointed out that moderate anxiety can sometimes have the effect of promoting fresh thinking and motivating a search for new and better solutions to the threat. However, he noted, if the anxiety becomes too severe, it tends to rigidify thought and paralyse initiative. Frank suggests that this may be somehow connected with the repetition compulsion in neurotics who keep on trying to solve current problems with outdated solutions: 'It may be that the neurotic is too anxious and demoralised to try something else; he finds it better to bear the ills he has than to risk new ones.'[1] At the level of group dynamics, a situation of tension is clearly reflected in the formation of enemy stereotypes: 'Whoever we are and whoever the enemy is,' says Frank, 'we gradually assume all the virtues and they become the incarnation of everything evil. It is frighteningly easy to create the stereotype.'[2]

Frank illustrates the frightening ease with which enemy stereotypes are created by citing an experiment which entailed setting up two groups in a boys' camp. Members of the groups did not know each other and competitive situations were arranged in which one or both groups felt frustrated. Within a few days each group had become a cohesive whole, bragging about its own virtues and having nothing but contempt for the other group.

15

Many psychological factors go into creating the bogey-man perception of the enemy, notably the convenience of projecting the sources of one's own tensions and frustrations and justifying one's own aggressive behaviour by the use of a scapegoat. The crucial question is why an enemy stereotype is so hard to break down, and what some of its consequences are likely to be.

It would seem that one's perceptions are largely determined by one's expectations or assumptions. This was neatly demonstrated in an ingenious experiment involving the use of an optical instrument called a stereopticon, which allows the experimenter to show different pictures simultaneously to the right and left eyes. When the device was used to show to separate groups of Americans and Mexicans a bullfighter and a baseball player, the Americans tended to see the baseball player and the Mexicans the bullfighter.[3] The observation that we see primarily what we want to see would appear to be empirically valid. As a direct result of this partial vision, there is a similar tendency to perceive nothing but darkness emanating from the enemy camp.

Frank also describes an experiment that was conducted with nineteen fifth- and sixth-grade American schoolchildren. They were shown photographs of Russian roads lined with trees, and asked why they thought these trees were growing alongside the road. Two of the most common answers given were: 'So people won't see what's going on beyond the road,' and 'It's to make work for the prisoners.' This is prejudice in the literal sense of the word: the accused is deemed guilty merely by virtue of being the accused.

Louis Halle, a journalist, noted how this kind of distorted jurisprudence is applied automatically at a psychological level:

> For Moscow to propose what we can accept seems to us even more sinister and dangerous than for it to propose what we cannot accept. Our instinct is to cast about for grounds on which to discredit the proposal instead of seizing it and making the most of it. Being distrustful of the Greeks bearing gifts, we are afraid of being tricked.[4]

Halle made this statement in 1959. The cold-war mould had already set by then and it has continued to harden. Clearly, the harder a mould has set, the more difficult it becomes to break. So even when we meet individual members of the nation perceived in demonic terms and find that they do not, after all, have horns and cloven hoofs, but appear to be, as Frank puts it, 'ordinary, easy-going, fun-loving family men like ourselves', we still tend to cling obstinately to prejudices and stereotypes by assuming 'either that they are diabolically clever at deceiving us, or that it is their leaders who are villainous'.[5]

Frank quotes from a letter he received in 1960, citing it as an example of the way enemy stereotyping can disrupt rational thought:

> One cannot reason, bargain, or do business with a Khrushchev any more than with a Hitler, except possibly at the end of a long club. The intent of this maniac is to enslave forever, to 'robotize' if you will, the entire human race. This fiend will consign humanity to an ant hill existence. Even the death of humanity is preferable to such an existence.[6]

The pronouncement 'better dead than red' can only apply if 'red' is perceived to be even more evil and diabolical than the final extinction of the species. Since it is rather difficult to envisage anything more evil than the latter, continued usage of this slogan gives one an idea of the strength of the cold-war doctrine. Although the concept may not normally be expressed in quite such lurid terms as those used by Frank's correspondent, it nevertheless remains the underlying assumption of cold-war philosophy and deterrent policy.

Since the enemy is viewed as diabolically clever, each side fears that the other would be able to use any improvement in communication to its own advantage. In November 1959, the US Senate Internal Security Committee called the Soviet-American cultural exchanges part of a 'poisonous propaganda offensive'.[7] At about the same time, the Soviet counterpart of this committee was warning that the Americans might use the programme as a 'Trojan horse'. Leaders on each side fear that their own people are so naive and innocent that they can be easily duped and misled. They believe any favourable information about the enemy is bound to be false. They expect the enemy would derive greater advantages from any exchange.

An even greater danger in mutual stereotyping is that it tends to bring itself about as self-fulfilling prophecy. An example of this can be found in the radical change in attitude towards mentally disturbed people. For many years psychiatrists expected all patients at mental hospitals to be violent and unmanageable. They arranged matters accordingly, locking patients in isolation cells, strapping them in chairs and imprisoning them in straitjackets. Predictably, patients were often violent and unmanageable. When the psychiatrists began to change their policies and expectations, they found that the patients usually fulfilled their more positive expectations. For example, out of nearly 1,000 patients admitted over a ten-month period, in a naval hospital, not one had to be restrained or put in isolation because the administrator of the ward had created strong positive group expectations.[8]

It is amply clear that self-fulfilling prophecies can be positive as well as negative. The negative psychology that has prevailed for the past forty years is reminiscent of the outlook of governors of Victorian asylums. Generally east-west relations have been conducted within the confines of the cold war straitjacket. The difference is that the inmates of the asylums were there against their will; we have created the cold war out of our own free choice.

Negative self-fulfilling prophecy often moves in a malignant direction: initially the assumed enemy may not in reality *be* so very untrustworthy. But if the mutual posture of mistrust persists long enough, assumed enemies eventually *become* untrustworthy, as each side acts in such a manner as to justify the other's suspicion. Frank refers to the 'melancholy sequence of events' following the downing of the American U2 spy plane in April 1960 as a typical example of this process in action: 'Each country takes steps, based on fear of the other's intentions, which, by heightening mutual distrust, increase the likelihood that the other will justify its pessimistic expectations.' The parallels with the Korean airline disaster in 1983 [9] and the shooting of the Iran Air plane in the Gulf in 1988 are obvious.

John Mack, a psychiatrist at the Harvard Medical School, observes:

> It is as if all through the presentation of the terrible information about how our civilization might be extinguished, one thought has been burning in the mind: 'What about the Russians?' as if somehow the evocation of the Soviet Union justifies anything.[10]

Yet, as Mack reminds us, despite all the cold-war rhetoric a strong bond exists between the United States and the Soviet Union: 'There can be no question of the absence of relationship, for we are deeply bonded to the Soviet Union.' It is only too easy to accept the facile and superficial image, disseminated and reinforced by the mass media, of two angry giants shouting at each other across a great divide of mutual incomprehension. But this is a false portrayal of what is actually happening at a deeper psychological level. A more apt analogy would be of two parents having a row under the same roof. The row is indicative of the bonding. Strangers do not usually have such intense rows with each other.

'The nuclear context has deepened and intensified the bond between the United States and the Soviet Union. The stakes in the relationship have increased,' Mack writes. Yet the bonding between the two superpowers is not a mutual relationship between equals; it is a geostrategic rivalry between two very insecure world powers.

Even the bonding of summitry seems to have produced only a more sophisticated hostility and an increasingly precarious world situation. Perhaps it is because summits are used more to influence domestic opinion than to solve international problems.

Charles Pinderhughes, Professor of Psychiatry at Boston University, has developed a concept, which he calls 'paired differential bonding', that connects psychology and physiology with social, political and cultural elements. He has shown that from an early age, as human beings form bonds with others, the brain creates two essential kinds of representation of the body and of the outside world. One type of bonding he terms 'A', or 'affiliative' bonding. A-bonding is reflected by closeness and affection. It relates to what is 'like me'. The second type, 'D', or 'differential' bonding, expresses awareness of what is different, or 'not me'. The first expression of differential bonding is seen in the anxiety infants feel toward strangers at around eight months.

Pinderhughes has used his theory of paired bonding to account for the tendency of people to divide the world into opposites and polarities with paired values – such as good and evil, light and dark, God and devil. The theory is applicable to both groups and whole societies: my group, my territory, my society, my religion are valued and idealized. The other society is not me in colour, language, religion, or political and economic system. It is devalued and, in extreme cases, dehumanized.[11] The Freudian psychoanalyst and social critic, Erik Erikson, calls the dehumanization of other groups 'pseudospeciation'.

Examples of pseudospeciation are plentiful. Many cultures (the Javanese, for example) even use the same word for members of their own group and 'human'. The Mundurucu of the Amazonian rain forest divide the world into themselves and the *pariwat* – everyone else – whom they regard as game to be hunted and speak of in the same terms that they reserve for peccary and tapir. Gary Trudeau illustrates a similar tendency in the cartoon strip *Doonesbury*. In one sequence BD went to Vietnam and was captured by a communist named Phred. At one point Phred gets a letter and BD asks, 'Who's that letter from?' Phred says, 'It's from my mother'. BD looks at the reader with a puzzled expression and says, 'I never knew commies had mothers.'

Frank observes that ethnocentrism – the overevaluation of one's own group in comparison with other groups, especially those perceived as rivals – is universal. Membership in a group is often an integral part of an individual's concept of himself or herself. The group's success is his or her success and its failures damage his or her self-confidence; its friends and enemies are also his or hers:

> Many people's group identification is so much a part of their personal identity that they would rather die than be absorbed into an alien group. Since everyone wants to think well of himself, he thinks well of his group – as far as he is concerned, the nation, class, or ethnic group into which he was born is the best, and he judges all events by its standards. Its world view is the correct one, its way of doing things the only proper one.[12]

This apparent willingness on the part of many people to fight rather than undergo a change in self-perception also forms one of the main ingredients of cold-war philosophy. It touches on something primitive and is therefore all the more powerful. In general parlance it is called patriotism.

———— 4 ————

Mirror images

THE TERM 'mirror image' was first applied to Soviet-American perceptions by the social psychologist Urie Bronfenbrenner in 1961 in a pioneering study. In the report he describes his own personal reactions to a visit to the Soviet Union in the summer of 1960, a time of more than usual tension, being only about a month after the U2 incident. During this fact-finding mission, in addition to visiting laboratories, universities and institutes, he also wanted to become better acquainted with 'living social psychology' – the Soviet people themselves. He spoke Russian and was also travelling on a visa which permitted him to go about freely, not always accompanied by an Intourist guide. After completing his official business at scientific centres, he spent several days just wandering about whichever city he happened to be in, striking up conversations with people in buses, parks, stores, restaurants, or just on the street. He found people very eager to talk and his many conversations with men and women of all ages convinced him that the majority of Russians feel a genuine pride in the achievements of their system.

Bronfenbrenner found his Soviet journey 'a deeply disturbing experience'. What frightened him was not so much the facts of Soviet reality as 'the discrepancy between the real and the perceived'. At first he was troubled only by the strange irrationality of the Soviet view of the world, especially the gross distortions of

American society and foreign policy. Then gradually it dawned on him with painful clarity that

> the Russians' distorted picture of us was curiously similar to our view of them – a mirror image. But, of course, our image was real, theirs based on propaganda. Or could it be that our view too was distorted and irrational – a mirror image in a twisted glass?

These seeds of doubt were to remain a frightening prospect: 'For if such reciprocal distortion exists, it is a psychological phenomenon without parallel in the gravity of its consequences'.[1]

Bronfenbrenner outlines some of the common features of the American and Soviet views of each other's society. He lists five main mirror-image themes:

1 They are the aggressors.
2 Their government exploits and deludes the people.
3 The mass of their people are not really sympathetic to the regime.
4 They cannot be trusted.
5 Their policy verges on madness.

Bronfenbrenner wondered why other western observers did not report the enthusiasm, the genuine pride in Soviet achievements and commitment to socialism which he found among the people there. When he discussed this with western journalists and officials at the American embassy in Moscow, one journalist put it to him: 'If I want to be sure my copy will be printed back home, I have to write about what's wrong with the system, not its successes.' The embassy officials implied that Bronfenbrenner was well intentioned but naive and gullible, and that he underestimated the effect of the police state: 'When these people talk to a stranger, they *have* to say the right thing.'[2]

This tendency to see only what you want to see has already been noted and it is a phenomenon well known to psychologists. New perceptions are assimilated into old ones and one unconsciously distorts what one perceives in such a way as to minimize a clash with previous expectations. As long ago as 1957, the social psychologist Leon Festinger proposed his important Theory of Cognitive Dissonance' in which the 'strain towards consistency' plays a central role. As we shall see, it is an especially powerful process in the sphere of social relations and in our perceptions of the motives and actions of other groups.

Such consistency is typically achieved by superimposing artificially simplified categories, most commonly the good/bad dichotomy. Once this has taken root, the rest falls into place: the 'good' group can have only desirable characteristics, while the 'bad' group can have only reprehensible ones. Bronfenbrenner states that

> when confronted with a desirable characteristic of something already known to be 'bad', the observer will either just not 'see' it, or will reorganize his perception of it so that it can be perceived as 'bad'. This tendency to regress to simple categories of perception is especially strong under conditions of emotional stress and external threat.[3]

This same oversimplified misperception has applied continuously throughout the duration of the cold war, in both directions.

What has become known as the 'Asch phenomenon' is a well recognized process, so named after some experiments conducted in 1956 by the social psychologist Solomon Asch. The subject finds himself or herself in a peer group of six or eight. Members are asked to make comparative judgements of certain stimuli presented to them – for example, identifying the longer of two lines. At first this seems simple enough; the subject hears others make their judgements and then makes his or her own. In the beginning he or she is usually in agreement, but then gradually notices that more and more often his or her judgements differ from those of the rest of the group. In fact, the other group members are plants and have been instructed beforehand to give false responses on a predetermined schedule. Finding himself or herself the odd one out has a dramatic effect on the subject; at first he or she is puzzled, then upset and soon begins to have serious doubts about his or her own judgement. In a significant number of cases the subject begins to 'see' the stimuli not as they actually are, but as described by his or her peers.

There is every reason to suppose, as Bronfenbrenner suggests, that the Asch phenomenon operates even more forcefully outside the laboratory 'where the game of social perception is being played for keeps'. He believes that exactly the same processes contribute substantially to producing and maintaining serious distortions in the reciprocal images of the United States and the Soviet Union. Such a suggestion is not made from abstract theoretical inference, but in this case as a direct result of Bronfenbrenner's own experience as its victim.

He spent as many hours as he could in a completely Soviet environment, trying, in so far as a westerner can, to perceive the world via Russian eyes. On one occasion he picked up a Soviet newspaper which featured an account of American activities in the Middle East and caught himself wondering what 'they' were up to now. He also found himself assenting to points made by Soviet friends, where previously he would have taken issue: 'When all those around me saw the world in one way, I, too, found myself wanting to believe and belong.'

On his way home to the States the process began to reverse itself and the more he talked with fellow Americans, the more he began to doubt his original impressions. The usual sceptical comments cropped up: 'How do you know you were not being followed by the KGB?'

Needless to say, mirror imaging also involves a strong element of self-fulfilling prophecy, which, as Bronfenbrenner warned, is possibly its most dangerous ingredient:

> Herein lies the terrible danger of the distorted mirror image, for it is characteristic of such images that they are self-confirming; that is, each party, often against its own wishes, is increasingly driven to behave in a manner which fulfils the expectations of the other . . . And as tensions rise, perceptions become more primitive and still further removed from reality. Seen from this perspective the primary danger of the Soviet-American mirror image is that it impels each nation to act in a manner which confirms and enhances the fear of the other to the point that even deliberate efforts to reverse the process are reinterpreted as evidence of confirmation.[4]

East-west relations tend to conform to the mirror image process. As tensions increase, mutual misperceptions grow increasingly primitive and move further and further from human reality. On reading Bronfenbrenner's 1961 report now, one has a strong sense of time standing still. Visitors to the Soviet Union today often go through the same sequence of feelings and impressions Bronfenbrenner outlined. They also tend to encounter precisely the same response from most other westerners on their return home: that they have been deceived by a cunning enemy, that all Russians are 'brainwashed', that any positive statements about the Soviet Union reflect gullible naivety, that all visitors are shadowed by the KGB.

The United States in fact has far more to lose during times of heightened cold-war tension than the Soviet Union. As Bronfenbrenner puts it:

> Internally the communist system can justify itself to the Soviet people far more easily in the face of external threat than in times of peace. And in the international arena, the more the United States becomes committed to massive retaliation and preventive intervention abroad, the more difficult it becomes for uncommitted or even friendly nations to perceive a real difference in the foreign policies of East and West.[5]

In the hall of twisted mirrors the truth becomes ever more elusive.

Among several positive suggestions for breaking the mould and preventing the process from getting completely out of hand, Bronfenbrenner suggests that the United States should whole-heartedly support exchange visits on a grand scale, set up conference centres, disseminate more objective information and revise immigration and travel restrictions, even in the absence of reciprocal actions by the USSR. As a preliminary gesture towards easing relations, he also suggests that the United States should close down some of its military bases abroad and turn over the space and buildings to more positive purposes, such as universities specializing in east-west relations, possibly under the auspices of the United Nations.

Even if the Soviet leadership initially dismissed them as mere propaganda, sooner or later the leaders would realize that they had made genuine gestures of reconciliation with no strings attached. They would then be likely to reciprocate in an equally positive manner, and the way could thus be opened to transform the vicious circle into a benign one. Had either superpower felt psychologically secure enough to have initiated such activities back in the 1960s, there is every likelihood that US-Soviet relations would by now have attained a far more balanced and more genuinely secure level.

Another major factor that contributes to the mirror-imaging process is the operation of a double standard. Over the years, both the United States and the Soviet Union have often taken similar, sometimes identical, actions. At various times both have increased their military budgets, both have made disarmament proposals, both have signed treaties and both have deployed troops in other countries. And yet, not entirely surprisingly, such US actions tend to be rated much more favourably by Americans than do identical Soviet actions. It can safely be assumed that a similar double standard prevails on the part of the Soviets. The assumption was methodically tested in 1965 by Stuart Oskamp, who provided a group of American college students with parallel 50-item questionnaires on US and Soviet actions. The students regarded most US actions far more favourably than identical Russian actions.[6]

Random, representative surveys and opinion polls have been repeatedly conducted over the years, probing attitudes towards Russia, China, Germany and Japan. Some of the surveys entailed selecting from a list of adjectives the ten that best described members of these other nations. In 1942, Germany and Japan were our bitter enemies and the Soviet Union was our ally. Among the first five adjectives then chosen to characterize the Germans and the Japanese were 'warlike', 'treacherous' and 'cruel'. None of these adjectives was at that time applied to the Soviets. By 1966, West Germany and Japan had become western allies and the hostile perception of the Soviet Union was by then well established. All these adjectives had disappeared from descriptions of the Germans and Japanese and now it was the Soviets' turn to be regarded as 'warlike' and 'treacherous'.[7]

On the other hand, in 1954 Lord Salisbury stated in the privacy of the cabinet room that he regarded the Americans as a greater threat to world peace than the Russians.[8] In Europe this view is now increasingly widespread. It is as if the demon image has hitherto hovered over humankind like a malignant satellite, constantly orbiting the earth until it is called upon to be beamed onto the enemy of the day.

The preservation of the national image is also part of the mirror-imaging process. Just as an individual ceases to think or act rationally while in the middle of a heated argument and the grip of strong emotions, in similar situations a whole nation's thinking becomes primitive. Fewer options are perceived, issues are grossly oversimplified and long-term consequences and implications for others are often not considered. At the time of the Falklands/ Malvinas conflict of 1982, the British war cabinet was so busy focusing on the sovereignty issue that it overlooked the possibility that the conflict could quite easily have escalated into a major confrontation, involving the possible use of nuclear weapons. As it was, there was talk of bombing the Argentinian mainland.

In the Wall Street crash of 1929 several financiers chose suicide, even though they still had plenty of money left, apparently because they could not bear to face the implications of their own faulty judgements. A strong motive for escalating the war in Vietnam was that the United States could not tolerate the prospect of being perceived as a 'weak and helpless giant'. The carnage of Verdun during the First World War provides yet another example. The battle raged on even after its strategic significance had long since passed out of sight: 'Yet the battle had somehow achieved a demonic existence of its own far beyond the control of the generals of either nation,' says the historian A. Horne. 'Honour had become involved to an extent which made disengagement impossible.'[9]

Since the groups and nations to which we belong are psychological extensions of ourselves, any intrusion on the physical or psychological integrity of a group is perceived by its members as a direct attack on them. When certain drivers respond with rage to a minor accident that damages their car, it is because the car is perceived as an extension of the driver and the slightest scratch to the car is seen as a huge dent in the driver's macho self-esteem. Hence the bumper sticker 'you toucha my car, I smasha your face'.

Under stressful conditions individuals may sometimes become more enraged by a slight to their group than to themselves, but groups may be more prone to rash actions than individuals. An individual may be restrained by other group members who do not share his or her perspective, while in a group reaction members may egg each other on, especially if emotion is already running high. Mutual reinforcement may be further strengthened by the process called 'groupthink', which we will be considering in the next chapter. The more the group feels threatened, the more its members are impelled to maintain group solidarity by kowtowing to their leader, even at the expense of their own more rational and objective judgements.

In an experiment in 1957 researchers directed groups of students to participate in stress interviews as well as in simple, completely painless procedures involving the use of electrodes. The researchers found that their subjects experienced more anxiety from the painless electrodes than they did from the stress interviews.[10] Fear of the unknown, of the uncertain, is often greater than fear of the known, even if the known involves pain and/or tension while the unknown might not necessarily involve either. It has been suggested by Berriman that

> mutual anxiety at the international level is greater when each country knows enough about the other to recognise that it has the power to inflict harm, but does not know enough to be sure of its intent or of how much power it actually has.[11]

What was described at the time (1985) as 'a startling break in Soviet attitudes to the west' appeared in the form of an interview with a senior Russian staff officer who works in Moscow as a researcher and commentator on international security. The officer told the interviewer that a combination of Russian 'mistakes' and western hysteria could be the fatal spark for World War 3. He stressed that there were no territorial disputes between the US and the Soviet Union, nor were there in reality any significant economic barriers. Mistakes in themselves need not be so very dangerous, he added, provided they are perceived at the time for what they are –mistakes, not part of some vast aggressive grand design. When asked whether he thought hysteria was a western monopoly, he replied that this was not what he intended to convey: 'In the past we have been able to keep a cool head. But we are also human and hysteria is an infectious disease.'[12]

5

Groupthink

'GROUPTHINK' is a term used to describe errors of decision-making that are based on a kind of 'frozen thinking' formed by two elements: a shared commitment based on group loyalty and allegiance to a leader. Within this rigid structure members of the group no longer think for themselves as individuals; their own critical faculties are suppressed in the interests of group conformity. Frozen thinking resists outside pressure to re-examine a pre-determined position in the light of subsequent important new data. The 'strain towards consistency' forms its most powerful ingredient.

The following are the main symptoms of groupthink elaborated by Janis and Mann in *Decision Making*, published in 1977:

1   An illusion of invulnerability shared by most or all members, which creates excessive optimism and encourages taking extreme risks.
2   Rationalization which precludes reconsideration of past decisions.
3   An unquestioned belief in the group's inherent morality.
4   Stereotyped views of rivals and enemies.
5   Direct pressure on any member who expresses strong arguments against any of the group's stereotypes, rationalizations or decisions.

6 Self-censorship of deviations from the apparent group consensus.

7 A shared assumption of unanimity.

8 The emergence of self-appointed 'mindguards' – members who protect the group from information which might question their consensus.

During the growing crisis between Britain and Argentina in early 1982, Mrs Thatcher and her war cabinet displayed all the signs of suffering from an illusion of invulnerability. The US Secretary of State Alexander Haig later remarked that she had cast herself in a 'messianic' role and as a result took decisions involving extreme risks. Warnings preceding the crisis were discounted or ignored, apparently blunted by an unquestioned belief in the inherent morality of the 'British position'. Anyone who was even remotely critical of the government's stand was quickly branded with accusations of treason. Rules of engagement were arbitrarily changed and the wider global and moral consequences of such decisions ignored.

The media was manipulated to create the enemy image of the 'Argies' with remarkable speed. This particular enemy also fulfilled the attribute of being regarded by the war cabinet as too evil, weak and stupid to warrant any attempts at negotiation. Besides, the 'task force' had sailed, the die had been cast.

Frank Heller, director of the Centre of Decision Making Studies at the Tavistock Institute of Human Relations, conducted some student projects on the Falklands/Malvinas war to test the Janis groupthink theory. The students produced evidence to support the presence of most of the eight symptoms listed above.[1] They concluded that though the Argentine aggression was morally wrong, it was based on rational sign reading. Their verdict on the British government was that groupthink prevented it from attaining a correct evaluation of the evidence. As Heller stresses, the whole point of a model like groupthink is that different critical situations do have a common core, a recognizable structure of decision-making 'which leads inexorably from plausible origins to ignominious outcomes'.

In practice, any kind of 'early warning groupthink watchdog committee', will be prevented from functioning effectively in the face of a group of decision-makers devoted to secrecy and to their self-importance. That is why those who make the most critical decisions are usually the ones to resist more open government, on the grounds that it would undermine 'national security'. It is only after a crisis is over that the people often learn that information they had every right to know had been withheld and that the facts would not have posed the slightest threat to national security.

The necessity for more open government becomes urgent when we consider that in the heat of a crisis decision-makers are hardly in a position to assess what is occurring at a deeper psychological level. Yet it is precisely these deeper processes that could critically affect decisions involving global consequences. It is easy to be wise after the event. But in a nuclear age wisdom must necessarily precede events.

Decisions are not taken by abstract entities, disembodied powers ('the government'), but by human beings of flesh, blood and feelings who work under increasing pressure as a crisis develops. The initial stages of a crisis can be stimulating, but as the pressure increases and the crisis deepens, serious disintegration of performance is likely. Detailed studies have been undertaken of the main phases the decision-makers go through, which the psychologist James Thompson summarizes as follows:

> Decision makers start to experience stress as the crisis develops. In the very early stages this may be pleasurable, since it gives politicians a sense of importance and expands their roles. They may enjoy the sense of teamwork that builds up as everyone gets to work. As the crisis deepens their thinking becomes polarized and oversimplified, with emotional overtones. They develop tunnel vision, becoming unable to see the other side's point of view. They give short-term objectives precedence over long-term goals, even though the short-term objective may run counter to what they wish to achieve in the long run. They find it difficult to generate a range of solutions to the problem, but tend to persist with the few they originally proposed, and find that they cannot anticipate counter-moves. Their powers of concentration begin to fail as stress builds up. Anxiety increases, mostly caused by uncertainty, and thinking becomes more rigid. Unity is seen as absolutely essential, and a

feeling of urgency pervades, in which delays in decision making are seen as fatal . . . Information from the other side is distrusted, and seen in a fear-distorted way, and as a consequence participants tend to respond with exorbitant bargaining positions, rather than realistic compromises, which thus makes the crisis worse.

It is a common experience of participants in a disastrous crisis that after it is all over they cannot understand how it all came about . . . The crisis takes on a life of its own because the participants are willing to believe in it, and take its urgency seriously. In a sense, most crises in history could be described not as 'follies à deux', but essentially as the madness of roughly two dozen people involved in the key war cabinets.[2]

Robert Kennedy, who was involved throughout, recalled the Cuban missile crisis in his book *Thirteen Days*. He said that, because of the pressure of events, some American and Soviet decision-makers appeared to lose their judgement and stability. Khrushchev's message of 26 October, 1962, never published, is said by some of those who have seen it to reveal the incoherence of a person on the verge of total emotional collapse.[3] The fact that we did not have a nuclear war in 1962 may be due more to good luck than to good crisis management.

————— 6 —————

The fortress of positivism

GROUPTHINK is not only a phenomenon that grips political leaders in crises. It represents an extreme form of something that is very common throughout society: namely, the coming together of individuals when they agree. People who share certain world views – such as a common religious outlook, or a political persuasion, or a particular athletic inclination – come together. In fact, societies become societies through a prevalence of common world views among the individuals that compose them.

Often the assumptions that bind people together are so deeply held that they remain unspoken. One question we must ask ourselves is: in what way does our societal outlook and general 'philosophy of life' connect with our military-strategic perception of the world? Without some kind of connection in outlook between the general public mind and the specific military mind, it would be difficult to explain how the 'defence' industry could consume so much of our resources with such widespread public support.

In other words, the general ethos or world view of our society – the way we ourselves commonly think and perceive the world – and the way the military mind operates are not dissimilar enough to make such cohabitation thoroughly dissonant and uncomfortable, if not unbearable. We have to burrow deeper than patriotism or the profit motive to explain the strange phenomenon of a culture supporting an enterprise precipitating its own end.

If we had to choose one word to summarize this connecting strand in our mental attitudes and outlook we would select the word 'positivism'. To be more specific, it is the 'Gradgrind' aspect of positivism that allows our society to coexist with the culture of potential omnicide it has produced. Gradgrind was that soulless character in Charles Dickens' *Hard Times* who had an obsession for facts, more facts and nothing but facts.

Obviously all scientific inquiry must be founded on a sound factual basis. What is objectionable is the denial of any other knowledge besides visible facts, as defined in reductionist terms. We are constantly exposed to visible facts, which are themselves the last links in long complex chains of causal processes, most of which are invisible and intangible and many of which are highly paradoxical in nature. But the 'Gradgrind' in us does not like these untidy paradoxes – he prefers a nice, neat, solid, visible fact.

The fortress of positivism lies at the centre of our western cultural world view. It is a world view shared by Soviets and Americans alike. It provides a link between the 'inner fortress' of the way we collectively perceive the world and the more visible and tangible 'outer fortress' of the scientific-military-industrial complex which we maintain against each other.

J.B. Priestley had this to say about the 'great central fortress' of positivism:

> This Fortress represents the greatest weight of authority known to us today. It is from here, not from Rome or any other religious centre, that the iron dogmas and decrees come. It is the citadel of science, technology, positivism . . . It is the home of science as a dogmatic system and a colossal vested interest. It is where most of the work, including the invention and development of nuclear weapons, is done. (How many maimed guinea pigs, cancerous rats, blind mice and infected frogs exist within these walls, we cannot imagine.) Its platforms and turrets are manned and grimly guarded by a gigantic army of theorists, researchers, experimenters, professors, teachers, technologists, publicists and journalists. Above the keep there flies the black and white banner of positivism.[1]

The positivist mentality, based as it is on non-paradoxical logical premises, distorts perception of the world and its inhabitants. An either/or mentality is fundamental to military strategy and the conduct of war: obviously the perceived enemy cannot be both hostile (unlike us), and yet at the same time human (like us).

The western prejudice against paradox has an ancient pedigree and can be traced back to the time of Plato and Aristotle. In our culture there is a tendency to see paradox as a bad thing, an obstacle in the way of 'logical thought'. This is part of our whole society's world view. We are simply not attuned to appreciating the potential value of contradictory facts existing simultaneously, or to understanding that it may actually promote a clearer perception of reality. The either/or dogma looks nice and neat, black and white, clear-cut and 'logical'. But it contains the seeds of its own unreason: it denies the fundamental psychological truth that contradictions exist in the internal world and the external world of human relations, creating a logic of paradox.

In an address to the American Psychological Association, the psychologist David Bakan explored some of the connections between war and the social sciences and listed some of the preferences with which positivism is generally associated:

> It prefers data to theory; and it prefers theory to speculation. It prefers data which are readily described physicalistically. Mentation and vitality, that is, mind and life, are not recognized. (Since life has no reality, killing and dying must have little significance.) . . . It avoids all questions of human values, seeking a 'value free' science . . . for positivism the only valid knowledge is that which is given by science, with physical science standing as its chief model. Physicalist facts are the only valued objects of knowledge. The positivistic position denies the existence or intelligibility of any other forces but physicalistic forces. Anything else exceeds the boundary of fact and scientific law. Any form of thought or procedure of investigation that is not reducible to the scientific method thus conceived is illegitimate. In the social sciences positivism expresses itself as behaviourism in psychology. It has also led to the redesignation of the social sciences as 'behavioural' sciences. It leads to the denial of mind, the failure to study it, and ultimately to mindlessness in practical action, by denying the effectiveness of mind in the world.[2]

Hiroshima represents the visible end product of a certain way of thinking that is culturally specific: our western world view. It also represents the ultimate in factual visibility. It is a fact so visible that the eyeballs of close witnesses melted. Faith in the concept of nuclear deterrence thus entails proportionate faith in the visible and physical and its accompanying denial of the invisible and metaphysical, of the more subtle and paradoxical aspects of life, the very processes that make us all human beings. A video society such as ours tends to prepare our culture to accept what could be termed 'the greatest visual spectacle on earth' as the ultimate 'show'. The problem is that we would not be alive to watch the show in question; we would have perished as part of it.

As Jonathan Schell observes, it is hard enough to envisage individual death but virtually impossible to envisage our own universal death. We are only able to *envisage* this event as spectators:

> Thought and feeling try to peer ahead and catch a glimpse of death, but they encounter their own demise along the way, for their death is what death is. In the same way, when we try to picture extinction we come up against the fact that the human faculties with which someone might see, hear, feel or understand this event are obliterated in it, and we are left facing a blankness or emptiness. But even the words 'blankness' and 'emptiness' are too expressive – too laden with human response – because, inevitably, they connote the *experience* of blankness and emptiness, whereas extinction is the end of human experience. It thus seems to be in the nature of extinction to repel emotion and starve thought, and if the mind, brought face to face with extinction, descends into a kind of exhaustion and dejection it is surely in large part because we know that mankind cannot be a 'spectator' at its own funeral any more than any individual person can.[3]

In our video culture as viewers we are continuously exposed to a visual behaviourist ideology – animated positivism. At the same time we are deluded into believing that we are merely passive spectators and that this passivity is completely normal under the circumstances. But in reality as viewers we are being continuously numbed by our very spectatorship. The long-running debate as to whether or not there is a causal link between violence on the screen and violent behaviour in everyday life is irrelevant compared to this disempowering aspect of the mere *act* of viewing, regardless of what is being viewed. It is how we view *ourselves* that ultimately counts - whether or not we connect ourselves with the outside world and its fate.

Symbolically, when we draw the curtains and settle down to an evening's viewing, we are not only voluntarily subjugating ourselves, we are also drawing the curtains on the outside world, cutting ourselves off from it. The idea that we may be sitting back while preparations are being made for the final curtain to fall on the world stage may even occur fleetingly to many of us, but for the most part we feel powerless to affect what seems to have taken on the aura of a dreamlike but natural phenomenon.

As Priestley observed, the mentality that produced the bomb in the first place was a positivist mentality. To the extent that we ourselves contribute to this metaphysically repressive mentality, we go on 'producing the bomb' in our minds.

———— 7 ————

'Specializing' the truth

WE HUMANS have a remarkable ability to adapt ourselves to situations we would never consciously choose. This quality is illustrated with painful clarity in an article published in the *Bulletin of the Atomic Scientists,* entitled 'Normalizing the Unthinkable', by Liza Peattie, a professor of urban anthropology at the Massachusetts Institute of Technology.[1] She draws a parallel between the collaboration in our society today to maintain our nuclear arsenals and the collusion in the concentration camps of Nazi Germany – a parallel that is hard to accept, for there is something in all of us that recoils at the thought. Surely we are better than *them.*

Peattie begins by pointing to a 1982 Environmental Protection Agency study of 'Evaluation Risks', which argues energetically against the 'panic image' of human behaviour in an emergency situation. It states that 'People will often stay in a potentially threatening situation rather than move out of it. Human beings have very strong tendencies to continue ongoing lines of behaviour in preference to initiating new courses of action.'

Peattie notes that current planning for the management of nuclear war in itself constitutes an exemplary confirmation of this principle. The situation which the planners address is the most horrendous conceivable. Yet the tone of the planning studies is entirely prosaic. Some government emergency planners use analogies with the familiar in the attempt to normalize the actualities they envisage in time of catastrophe. A study of the consequences of 'incidents' involving nuclear power plants draws from human actions and reactions in floods, fires and earthquakes. Information is drawn from deaths due to motor vehicle accidents, costs for food and housing, salaries and wages for National Guardsmen, policemen and firemen, loss of wages per day per evacuee.

Nuclear omnicide cannot be described by analogy to anything known. Yet planners resort to exploring the situation playfully, via models and games. One study Peattie cites declares that 'like war games and business games the post-attack problems from which a single city model might be used are characterized by both complex environments and incomplete sets of decision rules.' Such a gaming approach deals in 'weapons impacts', 'resource availability', 'cumulating costs of items or modules damaged beyond repair' and 'vulnerability indexes'. Dividing reduced resources by a greatly reduced population, the authors conclude that 'considering resources alone, a moderate level attack on the nation might reduce consumption to the equivalent of that of the Great Depression'. Ironically, says Peattie, the principle is correct. There appears to be no situation so abnormal – experimentally, socially, morally – that human beings, if alive and not totally stunned out of all ability to react, will not at least strive to assimilate to normal practice.

Even at Hiroshima, there became apparent a certain mad orderliness which we might interpret as the behavioural counterpart of the intellectual processes which would equate the effects of nuclear war with those of the Great Depression. In the words of Robert Lifton, survivors recalled that

> Those who were able walked silently towards the suburbs and the distant hills . . . They were so broken and confused that they moved and behaved like automatons. Their reactions had astonished outsiders who reported with amazement the spectacle of long files of people holding stolidly to a narrow, rough path when close by was a smooth, easy road going in the same direction. The outsiders could not grasp the fact that they were witnessing the exodus of people who walked in the realm of dreams.[2]

Consider human behaviour in the concentration camps, the most thoroughly studied phenomenon in recent times in which human beings normalized the unthinkable. Peattie points out that *Treblinka*, Jean-François Steiner's account of life in that concentration camp, describes how, even as the scale and atrociousness of the extermination process advanced, the institutions and social organization of the camp came more and more to parallel those of normal society. A prisoners' orchestra was formed and when the trains unloaded a new set of victims, musicians were pulled out of the ranks to join. Prize fights became another form of entertainment and another principle of selection. A park and a zoo were built.

Towards the end, when the Nazis began to realize that they were likely to lose the war, they began to conceal evidence. The prisoner-workers were set to operating heavy machinery to dig up bodies which had been piled into deep pits, so that they could be recovered and burnt. It took a little time to evolve the techniques for cremating this mountain of bodies, but eventually a regular procedure was developed, and the slow, smoky burning of the mass of old bodies became part of the normal functioning of the camp. Meanwhile a new institution came into being: a cabaret, shared by the Germans and some of the more established, and therefore privileged, inmates. Weddings were held and celebrated with festivities.

In the latter period of the camp's operation, the long-term inmates, now able to function on a more extended basis, began to organize an uprising. In Steiner's account of this process – which ended with a bloody battle and the capture and death of almost all of those prisoners who had escaped – the most painful part of the story is the difficulty experienced by the leaders in starting the revolt.

They kept putting it off, although they knew time was running short for them. They made calculations: the original Jewish population of Warsaw; the thousands who had passed through the gas chambers; the numbers that must be left; the weeks it would take to process the remaining Jews into extinction. They knew at the moment the death factory ran out of raw material that they too would go into the gas chambers. But no given day seemed quite

41

right. Steiner wrote that it was as if they were stuck in a dream: the dream of daily routine, of the normality of their behaviour. The camp, with its bureaucracy, its personalities, its roles, its burning bodies, its smoking chimneys, had become their total reality and they were unable to imagine anything beyond it.

Steiner's description of Treblinka is particularly rich in recording the process of normalizing an atrocious institution. There was the daily routine of blows, roll call and soup. There was the barter economy of bread, turnips, scraps of cloth, gold teeth. There were specializations: prison plumbers laid the water pipes in the crematorium and prison electricians wired the fences. The camp managers maintained the standards and ensured orderly process. The cobblestones which paved the crematorium yard at Auschwitz had to be perfectly scrubbed.

Despite the overwhelming tendency even among the victims to normalize the macabre, some reacted with a genuine search for meaning, like a flower pushing up through concrete. A particularly moving testimony of this comes from Victor Frankl, a concentration camp survivor who went on to become an eminent psychiatrist and the founder of logotherapy. His father, mother, brother and wife all died in camps or were sent to the gas ovens. On the face of it, from a positivist standpoint and by all the usual rules of non-paradoxical 'logic', he had nothing whatever to live for; his life would seem to have been totally devoid of meaning.

Yet in the very middle of the horror of this continuous death-immersion, Frankl found a form of inner liberation that proved to be his salvation. He describes in his book, *Man's Search for Meaning,* the paradox of finding inner freedom in the very midst of total repression:

> In spite of all the enforced mental and physical primitiveness of life in a concentration camp, it was possible for spiritual life to deepen. Sensitive people who were used to a rich intellectual life may have suffered much pain (they were often of a delicate constitution), but the damage to their inner selves was less. They were able to retreat from their terrible surroundings to a life of inner riches and spiritual freedom.

Frankl found that those with this capacity were able to survive while those without it tended to sink into depression and to die psychologically well before they died physically. He recalls:

> I remember two cases which bore a striking similarity to each other. Both men had talked of their intentions to commit suicide. Both used the typical argument – they had nothing more to expect from life. In both cases it was a question of getting them to realize that life still expected something from them; something in the future was expected of them. We found, in fact, that for the one it was his child whom he adored and who was waiting for him in a foreign country. For the other it was a thing, not a person. This man was a scientist and had written a series of books which still needed to be finished. His work could not be done by anyone else, any more than another person could ever take the place of the father in the child's affections.
>
> This uniqueness and singleness which distinguishes each individual and gives meaning to his existence has a bearing on creative work as much as it does on human love. When the impossibility of replacing a person is realized, it allows the responsibility which a man has for his existence and its continuance to appear in all its magnitude. A man who becomes conscious of the responsibility he bears towards a human being who affectionately waits for him, or to an unfinished work, will never be able to throw away his life. He knows the 'why' of his existence, and will be able to bear almost any 'how'.[3]

Peattie reminds us that it is often easy to forget that Germany in the 1930s was not a backward country. It was a world leader in modern music, philosophy, high technology and the social institutions we call the welfare state. To normalize the unthinkable, the world of the concentration camp had available to it not only the simple techniques of every human society – the establishment of routine – it also had technology and bureaucratic rationality. The inhabitants of Treblinka were able to normalize the atrocious by elaborating around it not only music and art, but also technology and management. Only a few, like Frankl, were able to maintain spiritual vision.

When we hear of 'scientific' experiments performed on inmates in the concentration camp setting we tend to recoil in horror. We must understand these experiments as arising not out of pure sadism, but out of that same human tendency to normalize any setting no matter how abnormal. It was quite in keeping with the spirit of it all that the 'experimental' medical tortures constituted the basis for papers read at scientific meetings where, although the source of the data must have been evident, apparently no protest was made. 'Science' in the concentration camp was yet another manifestation of the human normalizing tendency which came to link victims and torturers in the creation of a shared society based on the production of death. Nazi science was very positivistic.

Peattie observes that the Gestapo were masters at anaesthetizing language to hide their cruel intentions. They demonstrated what many now feel about the current nukespeak jargon, that officialese has a talent for discussing reality while denying it and calling truth itself into question. 'Special treatment' and 'special housing' were terms used to designate the gas chambers; 'disinfectants', 'materials for resettlement of Jews', 'ovaltine substitute for Swiss Red Cross' – all were references to Zyklon B gas. The sign over the gate of Auschwitz – 'Work makes free' – told with grim clarity the literal truth: 'Here we work people to death.' Behind this statement is the dreadful metaphysical admission: 'For us there is only one freedom – freedom to die.' 'To the Bath', said the sign pointing to the gas chambers and in fact the gas chambers and crematoria were kept spotlessly clean. 'Assigned to harvest duty' was the way one SS officer referred to his being assigned to Auschwitz. The double meaning of 'harvest' was doubtless not unintentional.

After the war, Soviets and Americans equated each other with the Nazis in a way that legitimized arsenals more deadly than anything Hitler had developed. No easy parallels can be drawn; we are left only with lessons to be learned today from how society adapted itself at the time to a dehumanizing technology. The Nazis are a case study of an entire society that lost its connectedness, its moral referent. People within it could act, but with no sense of responsibility, no human context. Their instincts seemed to allow them only to cover up their horror by becoming accustomed to it, anaesthetizing it behind clinical language while they gave in to the destructive power of what they had come to tolerate, accept and, for many, even to celebrate.

Peattie suggests that our techniques for dealing with nuclear weapons are roughly similar. We have a similar division of labour; similar structures of rewards and incentives, which encourage and support individuals to undermine daily, in countless small ways, the basis of common existence; and a similar system of bureaucratic formalism and of scientific and technological elaboration, to mask and legitimize what the technology really implies.

We are sceptical of the claims of 'good Germans' that they did not know what those crematoria were burning. Yet the American Catholic Bishop Leroy Mattiesen – now a particularly outspoken opponent of the nuclear arms race – served for nine years as a parish priest only two miles from the Pantex plant at Amarillo, Texas. He did not realize that its output was nuclear bombs. Pantex covers 10,000 acres and employs 2,400 people; it undertakes the final assembly of the entire United States nuclear arsenal.

Another central issue for war planners is the separation of planning from execution. Adolph Eichmann was a thoroughly responsible person, according to his understanding of responsibility. For him it was clear that the heads of state set policy. His role was to implement, and fortunately, he felt, it was never part of his job actually to have to kill anyone.

Peattie points out that the gradations of distance between conception and execution constitute varying levels of protection from responsibility and render the moral problem ambiguous. During the debates which took place in the late 1960s at Massachusetts Institute of Technology about its role in weapons development, the head of the main military research laboratory argued that its concern was the development, not the use, of technology. The university eventually undertook to sever operational weapons systems research from the Institute, but it still permitted on-campus work, which was funded mainly because of its potential military application.

Even while diffusing responsibility by separating planning from execution and divorcing one element of execution from another, the division of labour leads to complicity through the functional interdependence of the various parts of the process. In Treblinka, the Jews themselves had to become responsible for output as well as for discipline. Experience with the ghettos had taught the Germans that persons who had knowingly compromised themselves did not revolt against their masters, no matter what idea had driven them to collaboration.

The division of labour brings with it an organizational sociology of specialization, hierarchy and rewards. Material rewards are allocated on the basis of active and skilful participation in the system. Defence contractors can bid for the most skilled engineers and scientists and pay them generously. Weapons research and war planning become the path of material success. In the underworld of the concentration camp, the 'low numbers' – those who had survived for relatively long periods – were all specialists. Only they ate enough to keep alive.

The work-Jews at Treblinka ate relatively well and were relatively well-clothed because of the goods which came with the 'transports'. There are accounts of storerooms knee-deep in valuables. The transports of persons to the gas chambers were also the camp's lifeline. A survivor of Treblinka described how deep the economic base of complicity came to be:

> Things went from bad to worse that month of March. There were no transports – in February just a few, remnants from here and there, then a few hundred gypsies – they were really poor; they brought nothing. In the storehouses everything had been packed and shipped . . . And suddenly everything – clothes, watches, spectacles, shoes, walking sticks, cooking pots, linen, not to speak of food – everything went . . . You can't imagine what we felt when nothing was there. You see, the things were our justification for being alive. If there were no things to administer, why would they let us stay alive? On top of that, we were for the first time hungry. We were eating the camp food now, and it was terrible, of course, totally inadequate . . . In the six weeks of almost no transports, all of us had lost an incredible amount of weight and energy . . .
>
> It was just about when we reached the lowest ebb in our morale that . . . Kurt Franz walked into our barracks, a wide grin on his face. 'As of tomorrow,' he said, 'transports will be rolling in again.' And do you know what we did? We shouted, 'Hurrah, Hurrah'. It seems impossible now. Everytime I think of it I die a small death; but it's the truth. That is what we did; that is what we had got to. And sure enough, the next morning they arrived.[4]

Along with material success comes prestige. Salaries and positions translate into dinner parties with important people, heads turn when one enters the conference room. A former research analyst at the Department of Defence recalls:

> When I was chosen for a special clearance, my immediate feeling was one of achievement and pleasure. I also remember the earlier feeling when I was not cleared for special intelligence and how important it seemed to me to be one of the three or four who were cleared among the twenty or so analysts in the Political and Economic Section.[5]

Specialization brings with it the possibility of developing satisfaction in problem-solving, expertise and the exercise of skill. High technology is regarded by many of us as the creative frontier. The development of the atomic bomb is one of the great dramas of creativity of our time and the subsequent elaboration of the technology has provided, and continues to provide, opportunities for the intellectual excitement of stretching the mind to its limits.

The sense of joint discovery produces a profound feeling of community. Paul Loeb, studying the community that developed around plutonium production at Hanford, Washington, shows how the organizational process within the enterprise, and family and community life around it, give the production of bombs the most peaceful of settings. As one informant explained:

> We were proud to work for a major company like General Electric. We felt we were part of a well-run industrial enterprise with good management feeling because the AES (Atomic Energy Commission) would be comparing our cost and productivity figures with those of Savannah River. Some of us even went on recruiting trips, visiting colleges along with other people from GE divisions around the country – and we explained plutonium as simply our product, just as light bulbs and turbines were someone else's.[6]

Steiner makes a general point about Treblinka which seems relevant to the threat of nuclear omnicide. It is not simply the attachment to existing projects which makes it difficult to overcome; it is the very magnitude of the situation. An outcome of sufficient dreadfulness becomes, in effect, inconceivable. 'One fact played into the hands of the "technicians": the monstrosity of truth. The extermination of a whole people was so unimaginable that the human mind could not accept it.'

The enormity of nuclear omnicide plays a similar role in planning for civil defence. According to current plans, millions of people will gather their children; arrange to leave their pets with food and water; assemble shovels and clothing, and not forgetting credit cards of course. Then, affixing the proper civil defence stickers to their cars, they will move smoothly over bridges, through tunnels and down highways – normally clogged to a standstill by any holiday weekend – to pre-designated areas in smaller communities.

Nothing in this picture has any of the characteristics of an emergency situation. Indeed, to remove from the picture any semblance of a real nuclear war situation, all other real-world characteristics have also been removed. There are no traffic jams, no frantic parents searching for children, no wounded demanding urgent medical care. And what happens after the bombs have fallen, when the survivors emerge from the shelters with their credit cards intact? The plans offer neither description nor instruction.

It is fundamental for us to understand that the terrible sickness of the Nazi concentration camps emanated from ordinary people, incited by an extraordinary regime. That they were not so unlike all of us was demonstrated by their later trials which brought out their variety, their shades of character and even their capacity for change.

The final solution worked because the German people wanted it to work. Both government and public shared the German world view about German racial superiority and anti-Semitism. Instead of resisting it, rebelling against it, they put the best of their energies into making genocide a success – a truth that pertained not only to one or two psychopaths, but to an entire bureaucratic officialdom.

Although most war criminals argued that 'they had no choice' and that they were 'forced' to comply with orders, the war trials showed a more complex picture of the defendants. Almost all of them committed gratuitous acts of arbitrary cruelty and violence, which were forbidden even by the Gestapo's own rules. Some were even punished by the SS for these violations.

Was there no choice? There are on record refusals of men who simply would not take part in murder and got themselves transferred. Why was this not done more often? For one thing, Auschwitz was 'safe'. After all, one was not at the front and there was practically no danger from bombing planes. And there were privileges: the work was no doubt disagreeable to some, but there were extra rations, smokes, drinks. There also can be little doubt that some of these men and women tortured and killed because they actually enjoyed it.

A famous series of experiments has revealed that under the direction of the experimenter, two thirds of normal subjects were willing to administer electric shocks of apparently fatal voltages. So long as the experimenter was willing to accept responsibility for any injury sustained by the victim, most subjects continued to administer the shocks. The investigator, Milgram, came to the conclusion that the fundamental lesson in his study was that 'ordinary people, simply doing their jobs, and without any particular hostility on their part, can be agents in a terrible destructive process'.[7]

It is a sad conclusion that given the right situation, places like Auschwitz can today be set up, put into action and smoothly maintained, with thousands of people systematically starved, beaten, gassed and the crematoria going full blast. Such camps can be established at any time, anywhere and made to work with the greatest efficiency, because there seems to be no dearth of people who would be glad to do the job, *provided it is sanctioned by authority*. Many of us would submit to an ideology that sanitizes violence and destruction against guilt. For many of us it is enough to affirm one basic principle: anyone belonging to class X, or nation Y, or race Z is to be regarded as subhuman and consequently has no rights. All the rest falls into place without difficulty.

As long as this principle is easily available, as long as it is taken for granted, as long as it can be spread out on the front pages at a moment's notice and accepted by the majority, we have no need for monsters. Ordinary civil servants and good citizens will take care of everything.

—— 8 ——

Changing perceptions

HISTORY reveals the inexhaustible contradictions of human behaviour. They existed in the extreme conditions of the concentration camps. They also exist in the complexities of geopolitical relations. We have enormous capacity for both – co-operation as well as destructive competition. Moreover we also have the capacity to combine the two and engage in conflict by consent. The situation in south Asia offers an example. Here is one scenario; the Indian subcontinent, geographically, is an extension of the Asian part of the Soviet Union. Long ago the czars had their eyes on that landmass. Their designs and ambitions still survive. Soviet access to the Indian Ocean becomes even more pressing because of the US presence in Diego Garcia. The Soviets, by occupying Kabul, gave the United States a valid reason to arm Pakistan. That made the rulers of India nervous. They began to scour the world for 'counter-balance arms' to defend their borders, should the need arise.

The Soviet presence in Afghanistan started an unprecedented arms race in South Asia. The Soviets, not happy at the Indian efforts to procure arms from whatever source they could, leaked out the Bofors 'irregularities'. As a result, western arms suppliers became wary of Indians and doubted their reliability. So the Indians had to go back to Moscow. In welcoming them back into the fold, Moscow demanded and obtained the price which could bring about the realization of the original czarist dream: Russian access to the Indian Ocean.

Indians had supported the Tamil separatists of Sri Lanka for a number of years. Yet, just before the signing of the INF treaty in Washington, the Indian government joined hands with the government of Sri Lanka against the Tamil Tigers it had nurtured for so long. An accord was signed which excluded the very people it was supposed to protect. The Tamils in Sri Lanka and the Indian Peace-keeping Forces lined up against one another in that former island paradise. The Tamils have spread (or been allowed to spread) from their strongholds in the north and northeast all over the island. In other words, the 'cancer' that was contained in one limb now afflicts the entire body. This will make it necessary for India to 'police' the island for a long time.

During that period, under pressure from India, the leaders in Colombo will be encouraged to sign a defence treaty with the Soviet Union. The text of a treaty for collective security of South Asia has existed since the Brezhnev days.

It is unlikely that such a shifting of alliances would have suddenly occurred without at least the tacit agreement of the other super-power. The compulsions that lead us into such shifting alliances raise profound questions about 'human nature'.

If we start from the premise that we humans are by nature ruthlessly competitive, then the very idea of co-operation seems highly unrealistic. Similarly, if we perceive the species as a whole in fatalistic terms – 'war is in our nature' – then we make trust the first casualty of human relations. Yet if we were solely aggressively competitive the whole planet would have been destroyed long ago. It is also clear that we are not totally altruistic beings. The only assertion that can be made with any degree of certainty is that we are by nature highly paradoxical – containing a variety of contradictions simultaneously.

An ultra-pessimistic image of humankind is essential to cold war doctrine and its accompanying deterrent policy. As this perception has come to permeate our culture, the more positive aspects of our nature and our creative and co-operative potentials have largely been eclipsed.

Patrick Bateson, Professor of Ethology at Cambridge University, gave an address on co-operation in 1985 which opened as follows:

> I am disturbed by the way we have created a social environment in which so much emphasis is laid on competition – on forging ahead while trampling on others. I dislike the way our country is divided by confrontational politics and I am frightened when this same style is used in international affairs. The ideal of social co-operation has come to be treated as high-sounding flabbiness, while individual selfishness is regarded as the natural and sole basis for a realistic approach to life. The image of the struggle for existence lies at the back of it, seriously distorting the view we have of ourselves and wrecking mutual trust.[1]

Bateson went on to observe that the fashionable philosophy of individualism claims respectability on the basis of a highly selective view of Darwinian theory:

> It is the Darwinian concept of differential survival that has been picked up and used so insistently in political rhetoric. Biology is thought to be all about competition – and that supposedly means constant struggle. This emphasis has had an insidious effect on the public mind and has encouraged the belief in individual selfishness and in confrontation. Competition is now widely seen as the mainspring of human activity, at least in western countries. Excellence in the universities and in the arts is thought to be driven by the same ruthless process that supposedly works so well on the sportsfield or market place, and they all have a lot in common with what supposedly happens in the jungle. The image of selfish genes, competing with each other in the course of evolution, has fused imperceptibly with the notion of selfish individuals competing with each other in the course of their life-times. Individuals only thrive by winning. The argument has become so much a part of conventional belief that it is hard at first to see what is wrong with it.[2]

Bateson cites examples of co-operation throughout nature, from lichens to birds and mammals, concluding that 'co-operation among social animals belies the myth of constant struggle'.

Karl Marx's collaborator, Friedrich Engels, was one of the first to spot the blatant political opportunism involved in selecting certain bits from early evolutionary theory and using them to justify the ruthless competitiveness of a capitalist economy. Such notions would initially be exported from political economy to biology, then reimported as 'natural laws' of social life: 'The puerility of this procedure', wrote Engels in 1875, 'is so obvious that not a word need be said about it.' But plenty more was said about it, and social Darwinism became a powerful political movement in the late nineteenth century.

In his 1980 Darwin Lecture to the British Association, the biologist John Durant explored what he aptly referred to as the 'beast in man myth', stating that 'the influence of the idea of the beast in man in the twentieth century has been enormous'.[3] He traces the course of the myth – which could be described as a rebirth of the Christian doctrine of original sin in more secular attire – through the theories of the early evolutionists, Galton and notably Darwin himself, via Freud and his theories of innate aggressive instincts, down to modern popular ethologists such as Lorenz, Ardrey and Morris.

The main focus of Durant's critique is the way in which aggression is almost invariably treated as a natural entity, a 'thing' in its own right:

> Whether it is Darwin discussing the devil under form of baboon, Freud contemplating the biogenetic origins of human warfare, Maclean hunting for the 'paranoid streak in man', or Tiger developing 'an almost medical conception of aggressiveness as epidemic, contagious and anti-vital', the idea of the beast in man always treats aggression as a natural entity.[4]

The real issue is not the source of our aggressiveness – whether from nature (genes, drives, instincts, etc.), or nurture (environment, learning, society, etc.). The issue is why we have elevated aggressiveness to be the most fundamental element of human behaviour. Its interpretation as only one dimension of our highly complex biology and culture with specific personal, social and political significance seems to have been banished to some romantic past that is out of key with the hard-edged 'natural laws' of today.

Over the past two decades, reductionist attempts to apply narrow simplistic theories of human nature have met a rising tide of criticism. The basic argument has been that particular views of society are projected into nature and then recovered in a more powerful naturalistic form. As Durant puts it:

Where this occurs, the mythical and ideological character of science is fairly obvious . . . and it is a depressing fact that it is far easier to find biological perspectives being used to set pessimistic limits to what is humanly possible than it is to find them operating in a context of optimism and encouragement. Since what people believe to be possible is part and parcel of what is actually achieved, it is hard to deny the justice of the radical objection at this point.[5]

Durant goes on to assert that Freud moved towards his increasingly pessimistic theory of human nature as a direct result of the First World War. When Dart came to interpret his fossils, he started from a pre-existing position of extreme pessimism: 'the loathsome cruelty of mankind to man' – a cruelty to which the 'blood-bespattered, slaughter-gutted archives of human history from the earliest records to the most recent atrocities of the Second World War' bore eloquent testimony. Lorenz wrote in similar terms about the aggression drive in the heart of man, inherited from his anthropoid ancestors.

Durant suggests that in each case the idea of the beast in man is the result of an era that seemed to demand a direct response to the problems of violence and warfare. This is why the pop ethologists were best sellers towards the end of the sixties. A whole series of prominent issues, from the growth of violent crime to the Vietnam War and the continuing escalation of the arms race, served to focus attention on the problem of human aggression. The context of the time encouraged a search for sweeping solutions to social problems, 'a context within which almost any scientifically plausible theory claiming to explain the reasons underlying people's alienation from one another and from nature was guaranteed to obtain a good hearing'.[6]

The results of the attempts of the pop ethologists to derive insights relevant to contemporary problems from the theory of evolution were inevitable: the theory became a self-reflecting mirror which reflected *only* those aspects of human experience which its authors wanted to stress. It was perhaps only to be expected that in an age of total war, our earliest ancestors should be portrayed as savage killers who rose to dominance in the natural world through their love of slaughter. 'This is precisely what we would expect of a scientific myth', writes Durant, who goes on to observe that

> Dart's interpretation of Australopithecus has been completely superseded by more recent studies of the fossil material; Lorenz's method of making free-wheeling comparisons between the behavior of fish, birds, mammals and people has been discarded by most of his scientific colleagues; and Ardrey's books have been safely consigned to the section of the library shelves marked fiction.

But the harm has been done. The massive publicity given to the pop ethologists, reinforced by the evangelical and fundamentalist Christian proclamation of human depravity because of original sin, was out of all proportion to the simplistic quality of their sweeping claims. The public mind was imprinted with the 'discovery' that our own species, and therefore all our fellow humans, are by nature bloodthirsty and totally untrustworthy.

Such primitive perceptions are tailor-made to justify cold-war policy. Within such unbalanced and ultra-pessimistic perspectives, deterrence seems to be the *only* realistic strategic option. All attempts at improving communication, bridge-building and establishing mutual trust appear to be flying in the face of 'reality' and 'human nature'. It has therefore become popular in certain quarters to regard such conciliatory gestures as well-intentioned but basically misguided and naive.

Clearly, what we now need is a change in perception so radical that the very idea of not co-operating with each other on a small planet faced with the common global enemy of total destruction is seen to be utterly inconceivable. Compelling and obvious though this fact may be, it does not yet seem to supply enough motive power for us to perceive co-operation as an absolute necessity and for us to insist on its practical implementation at the highest levels of policy-making.

Perhaps an allegorical tale might help us see ourselves more clearly. The story is told by Haniel Long in his inspiring epic, *The Marvellous Adventure of Cabeza de Vaca.*[7] Nuñez Cabeza de Vaca was leader of an ill-fated expedition of Spanish *conquistadores* to Florida in 1528. He was one of the few survivors washed ashore somewhere in the Gulf of Mexico. He led two other Spaniards and a

Moor on a journey across the entire continent which took them eight years. At first, the Indians thought that these white men were emissaries of the gods and thus equipped with supernatural healing powers. When the strangers denied that they had such powers, the Indians issued a stark ultimatum: 'Heal our sick, or die'. This greatly concentrated the minds of the *conquistadores*, who began praying and invoking Christ's name. To their amazement, some of the sufferers seemed to recover. Thereafter they were accepted by the Indians. Nuñez observed, 'Being Europeans, we thought we had given away to doctors and priests our ability to heal.' They grew to respect the Indians and their way of life to such an extent that they underwent profound inner changes, radical shifts in perception.

The hardest thing of all for Nuñez – far more difficult than all the starvation and privation – 'lay in parting little by little with the thoughts that clothed the soul of a European, and most of all the idea that a man attains strength through dirk and dagger'. When Nuñez met some *conquistadores* who had been laying waste the land and enslaving the people, he wrote: 'In facing these marauders, I was compelled to face the Spanish gentleman I myself had been eight years before.'

The real point of the story and why it is relevant to us today is that, as a direct result of seeing the human qualities in others previously perceived as enemies, or as mere subhuman objects, Nuñez and his companions underwent radical transformations in perception: 'We were more than we thought we were. To be more than I thought I was – this was a sensation utterly new to me.'

----- 9 -----

The new diplomats

THE STORY of Nuñez expresses a recovery of the original healing role of diplomacy. In ancient times the symbol of Hermes' caduceus, similar to the staff of Asclepius but with two snakes instead of one coiled round a central pillar, was used by envoys to ensure their safe passage. Today, diplomats are international bureaucrats rather than healers.

While the information explosion has made more and more information accessible to us citizens, it has also provided its main suppliers (governments) with an ever-increasing area of influence. This power of information has frequently been abused, more for disinforming, misinforming, selective leaking, or, like a tree in a forest, hiding correct information in the midst of incorrect, not quite so correct, or even correct but irrelevant information.

However, one piece of vital information that has filtered through to the collective psyche of the public at large is that the concept of the nation-state no longer applies in the 'global village' of modern technology.

Today, no Soviet soldier need land on American soil to stage an attack. The modern counterparts of Marco Polo have no need to trek all the way to China to discuss a possible spaghetti deal. War business and other kinds of business can all be conducted from remote bunker or comfortable office. At the press of a button, a battery of missiles carrying the most lethal weapons designed by humans can speed through space to mount an attack. Press another button and, via the miracle of technology, links will instantly be established to talk with and listen to people around the world. The so-called 'secure boundaries' that seemed so essential for national survival before the advent of the nuclear age have now become not only irrelevant but redundant. For the first time in recorded history, humankind is becoming aware of its oneness, more aware that 'the other' is ourselves, that 'them' is us, that we all inhabit a relatively small and very vulnerable planet. Those who profit most from distorting, diluting or delaying this awareness keep propagating the old images – us and them, US and SU.

The event of the signing of the INF treaty in Washington in 1988 was broadcast live to all corners of the earth in an attempt, as it were, to reassure the human race that its future was no longer threatened. It was said that for the first time the two superpowers were actually eliminating weapon systems. Within twenty-four hours of the much-publicized event in Washington, news reports were not only hinting but clearly spelling out that the two sides and their allies were looking at various ways and means of 'compensating' the losses that the treaty would entail.

Whether or not this particular treaty will make the world a safer place to live in remains to be seen. What this event tells us yet again is that the signing of treaties, no matter how pious and noble the intentions, is not enough. Treaties are signed between governments, not people. Though governments claim to represent people, the facts belie this claim. The people who have been let down by their own governments far more often than by 'enemy' governments are now at last beginning to assert their own power.

Remarkable as it may seem, given the present levels of international hostility, healing is taking place and with it a new sense of the potential of human co-operation is developing. While governments contrive to arm, spiritual awakening is in progress and it is having a direct political impact, even in the seemingly intractable arena of Soviet-American relations. For the first time, numerous private citizens and organizations have begun to incorporate international diplomacy into their sense of personal responsibility. They have become diplomats – citizen diplomats –

and are in the process of breaking down stereotypes of 'the enemy', shattering the barriers of groupthink and mirror imaging, and demonstrating that human beings can be as co-operative as they have been combative.

In Europe also a new diplomacy is emerging. In western Europe, the old post-war consensus about the cold war and the assumed need for a nuclear shield against the Soviets has been seriously questioned. The Green movement has made its power felt not only in West Germany, but in other countries as well. In eastern Europe, the spirit of Solidarity continues to live despite attempts to destroy it. In the midst of ancient antagonisms and complex enmities, a new fraternity is emerging.

The American citizen diplomats, the West German Greens and the Polish Solidarists are very distinct in their roots and very different in terms of the political contexts in which they work. But they have a great deal in common in the quality of their world views and in the nature of their commitments.

Citizen Diplomats[1]

Joseph Montville, a career diplomat and Research Director of the Center for the Study of Foreign Affairs at the US State Department's Foreign Service Institute, coined the term 'track two' diplomacy in 1982 to describe citizen initiatives between nations. Track two refers to constructive, unofficial, informal interactions between individuals and groups on different sides of ideological, ethnic and sectarian conflicts. Conceived as an adjunct to track one diplomacy (which refers to official, traditional, nation-to-nation channels), track two seeks to reduce psychological barriers between contending parties, creating new possibilities for negotiation on more formal levels.

Montville points out that political leaders are like tribal chiefs. They must assure their followers they will defend them against aggressors. Even the most sophisticated leaders must adopt forceful postures at crucial moments to meet this most primitive and enduring need of people living in groups. The problem is that this necessary and predictable posturing often provokes groups into going to war. Concrete political or economic grievances, compounded by historical and cultural factors, often lead to misperception and thus to lost opportunities to resolve differences before the fighting begins. The existence of a second diplomatic track can therefore provide an indispensable path to supplement the sometimes narrow limitations of official relations, especially in times of tension. If it is the role of leaders to defend, it can be the role of certain citizens to extend a hand of friendship.

Track two diplomacy, because of the nature of its unofficial, non-structured interactions, can afford to be 'strategically optimistic', to use the words of the Harvard social psychologist Herbert C. Kelman. Its underlying assumption is that actual or potential conflicts can be resolved or eased by appealing to common human capabilities to respond to goodwill and imagination. Montville notes that 'reasonable and altruistic interaction with foreign countries can be an alternative to track one diplomacy, with its official posturing and its underlying threat of the use of force'. What needs to be emphasized, he believes, is that 'both tracks are necessary for psychological reasons and both need each other'. In fact, he adds, 'people may respond more readily to track two diplomacy if they are first reassured that their leaders will defend their interests'.[2]

Sending private emissaries either overtly or covertly to foreign lands has been a recognized tool of diplomacy for perhaps as long as diplomacy has existed. It has been essential to the conduct of diplomacy during cold-war periods. After the Second World War, for instance, President Eisenhower, feeling blocked at the level of government-to-government communication, sent Norman Cousins, then editor of the *Saturday Review,* to discuss with the Soviets what private citizens representing a broad range of American public opinion could do to help ease tension between the two superpowers. Cousins journeyed to Moscow, where he discussed the idea of such a US–Soviet dialogue with Soviet officials. Several considerations led him to believe that unofficial, informal and private gatherings would be an effective way to build personal rapport that will transcend ideological differences. Official negotiations, mainly on disarmament, had yielded little in the way of substantive agreements. Perhaps even more important to Cousins was his belief that in the nuclear age the vital questions of the future of humanity were too important to be left to governments. It was time, he believed, for private citizens to contribute in a responsible way to the dialogues between nations on issues of peace and security.

The timing for such a suggestion was right. Eisenhower and Khrushchev had signed a cultural exchange agreement in 1958, and Khrushchev quickly agreed that the Soviet Peace Committee would take up Cousins' proposal under this larger orbit. In the United States, the Ford Foundation, a principal sponsor of several private activities already in progress under the 1958 agreement, decided to finance the experiment, while US planning responsibility was left to a committee headed by Cousins.

The first session of the formal talks took place on the campus of Dartmouth College in Hanover, New Hampshire, in 1960, during the last months of the Eisenhower administration. It was sufficiently well received by both nations to lead to a continuing series of full conferences and small task forces being convened. These Dartmouth Conferences constitute the most established continuing exercises in bilateral communication between Soviets and American citizens since the Second World War.

Individuals have also been called upon to help mediate crises. In 1978, President Carter called upon Dr Olin Robison, President of Middlebury College, to help negotiate the exchange of two American-held Soviet spies and five Soviet dissidents. This exchange marked the first time an American negotiator traded Soviets for Soviets. Robison's success in this role laid the basis for another task: securing a negotiated settlement for thirty-two Soviet Pentecostalists who had taken refuge in the American Embassy in Moscow. He began negotiating with the Soviets on behalf of President Carter and continued to do so on behalf of President Reagan. In 1982, a resolution was obtained: the Pentecostalists left the Embassy and went home as the Soviet government required. Thirty-one of them were then given exit visas, which had been the original purpose of their visit to the embassy.

The increase in citizen diplomacy since 1980 has its roots in what had gone before. It has also been motivated by the inability of governments to deal effectively and/or creatively with major problems such as the arms race. The accessibility of government to citizens in the West, and their freedom to travel to the Soviet Union, has been a major element in the growth of this movement. What makes the recent track-two diplomacy remarkable is that the citizen diplomats have not been limiting themselves to supporting or mediating government policies. Citizen diplomats from America have been setting their own agendas, careful not to antagonize the government, but nevertheless remaining clear that they have a responsibility to create their own relationships and programmes with the Soviets, to which their government can respond rather than dictate.

This kind of citizen diplomacy is in fact the culmination of an historical process that began at the close of the Second World War when the American government dropped two atomic bombs on Japan. Most citizen diplomats were born after the war. As adolescents, they were witnesses to the civil rights movement; they came of age during the Vietnam War. While their parents had faith in government, born out of government successes in the New Deal and Second World War, those who were born after the bomb had a very different experience as they encountered a series of government failures. The Vietnam War marked the first war in history when young men *en masse* refused to fight. After Vietnam came Watergate, and after Watergate the recognition that not only was extensive environmental pollution occurring but that the government arsenals and nuclear strategies were out of control.

This awareness triggered the resurgence of the anti-nuclear movement of the 1970s and the physicians' movement of the early 1980s, catalysed by Dr Helen Caldicott who began a world-wide campaign to educate the public about the medical and biological effects of nuclear war. In turn, this led to widespread discussions about the Soviet Union, for in the public mind the nuclear issue and the Soviet issue are but two sides of the same coin. Any real discussion of bomb blast, fallout or nuclear winter inevitably leads to the response 'What about the Russians?'

It was this combination of concerns that formed the impulse for current citizen diplomacy. Citizens concerned about the nuclear crisis began to travel to the Soviet Union to discover for themselves who these people were.

They discovered in the Soviets what Nuñez had discovered in the Indians of North America. The Soviets, while certainly ruthless and bureaucratically rigid in many ways, were also friendly, intelligent and devoted to working towards visions of the future remarkably similar to those nourished by the citizen diplomats. Across the Soviet spectrum the Americans uncovered an extraordinarily complex culture and people who wanted to begin working creatively together with them. In short, the new citizen diplomats discovered the humanity of the people who exist behind the harsh aspect of the Soviet political system. And because they did not go as tourists, but as citizen diplomats who carried a new message about America and a willingness to accept the Soviets as equals, they met with a warm and constructive response.

What is particularly innovative about these new track-two diplomats is that their activities have covered the whole gamut of issues and concerns. Esalen Institute's Soviet-American Exchange Program, for instance, evolved out of the human potential movement. Contacts with like-minded colleagues in the Soviet Union generated more contacts, initially in the fields of psychical research and exceptional human performance but then increasingly in areas as diverse as astronaut–cosmonaut dialogues, health promotion, satellite communication, literature, political psychology, and economics.

The Institute for Soviet-American Relations (ISAR), based in Washington DC, grew out of Esalen's initiatives. Its first project was to catalogue the US organizations that are engaged in citizen diplomacy – some 300 in 1988 – an astounding number given the fact that barely a dozen significant organizations were so involved at the beginning of the Reagan administration in 1981. Several organizations offer examples of the breadth of the current wave of citizen diplomacy activity. Internews has developed the field of spacebridges – using satellites to allow Soviets and Americans to communicate directly. The San Francisco-Moscow Teleport has pioneered computer link-ups. Search For Common Ground has developed a Soviet-American Taskforce on Terrorism. The US-USSR Youth Exchange has sponsored a series of wilderness adventure treks in the Caucasus Mountains for young Soviets and Americans. The Harvard Nuclear Negotiation Project explores how negotiation can reduce the risk of nuclear conflict.

These projects are only the tip of the iceberg. The quarterly journal of the Institute for Soviet-American Relations, which itemizes the activities of citizen diplomats, now runs to over one hundred pages. Americans from virtually every profession and walk of life are travelling in unprecedented numbers to the Soviet Union with the intention of visiting and developing working relations with their Soviet counterparts. A variety of new organizations has sprung up, such as the Center for US–USSR Initiatives, which works to organize group visits to the Soviet Union. The numbers of people who travel to the USSR under its and similar organizations' auspices run into the thousands and come from across the United States. Dozens of Soviet and American cities have twinned successfully. The demand has become so large that several travel agencies have been set up exclusively to service citizen diplomats.

In Europe, a similar phenomenon is occurring. The UK-USSR Medical Exchange Programme, which grew out of the Medical Campaign Against Nuclear Weapons, conducts a regular exchange with Soviet doctors. An east-west group of the German Green Party facilitates dialogues between Soviets and West Germans. European Nuclear Disarmament (END), a Europe-wide movement, links peace groups in the NATO bloc with human rights groups in eastern Europe and with the Group to Establish Trust between the USSR and the USA in the Soviet Union. Almost every NATO country has a host of similar private initiatives seeking to improve east-west understanding. The 1985 Nobel Peace Prize was awarded to the International Physicians for the Prevention of Nuclear War (IPPNW), founded by Bernard Lown, a Harvard cardiologist, and Evgeny Chazov, Minister of the Soviet Ministry of Health. IPPNW has 150,000 members in over fifty countries around the world.

These activities are all taking place in the midst of tremendous changes in the western public's perception of the nuclear threat and consequently attitudes towards the Soviet Union. While they continue to support a nuclear arsenal, for instance, Americans no longer believe as they once did that nuclear war is winnable and survivable. A 1955 Gallup Poll found that only a quarter of the public (27 per cent) agreed that 'mankind would be destroyed in an all-out atomic or hydrogen bomb war'. By 1961, a much larger minority (43 per cent) had come to feel they would have a poor chance of surviving such a war. In 1984, a two-thirds majority (68 per cent) held this view.

In part this change reflects America's revised understanding of the relative strengths of the United States and the Soviet Union. When the United States alone had the bomb, most Americans had few doubts about their safety. After the Soviets achieved nuclear status, and even after they developed the hydrogen bomb, Americans' confidence in their nuclear superiority still provided a feeling of security. Today, only 10 per cent of Americans believe America has nuclear superiority. A majority now feels that the two superpowers are roughly equal in destructive capability at a level felt to be terrifying. Polls indicate similar feelings among America's NATO allies.

Subtle but far-reaching changes have also taken place in the thinking about communism amongst the peoples of the Atlantic Alliance. Beyond the McCarthy period and well into the 1960s, Americans expressed fear that communism might spread, not only in the USA but also among its allies in Europe. Communism was viewed as a monolithic ideology that threatened freedom everywhere. Today, Americans, in common with the Soviets, have reached a position on communism that can best be described as pragmatic rejection. As they have in the past, Americans firmly reject the values of communism and see them as opposed to everything their own country stands for. But there is little fear today that communist subversion threatens the USA. In fact, a Public Agenda survey in 1984 showed that an overwhelming majority of the public concurred that 'our experience with communist China proves that our mortal enemies can quickly turn into countries we can get along with' (83 per cent). The belief that communism is something Americans can tolerate without endorsing represents another, and perhaps fundamental, shift in the public's thinking since the beginning of the nuclear age.

What the polls seem to indicate about American perceptions of the Soviets is that while the two political cultures represent fundamentally different value systems, war is simply not an option for settling those differences. Similar poll results exist in western Europe. Nuclear weapons are forcing us to begin to live with our disappointments in one another. They are compelling us to explore these co-operative aspects of our humanity rather than just the competitive ones.

The initiatives of citizen diplomacy are therefore directly linked to the psychology of the nuclear era. In the midst of traditional antagonisms nuclear weapons impel us to explore creative solutions. It is the purpose of citizen diplomacy to change the symbiotic relationship between the leader and the led by seeing international relations as an area where personal initiative can bring positive results. By engaging Soviets, Americans and Europeans in endeavours which not only bring them together as equals but in a way that benefits all sides, citizen diplomacy is creating the type of psychological context in which governments can be compelled to define security as not only defence of national interests, but also integration of national interests.

This does not mean that citizen diplomacy emphasizes only aspects of commonality between Soviets and Americans, while ignoring the differences. On the contrary, in dealing with the Soviet people it is important to understand that while at one level Americans and Soviets share a common humanity, at another level fundamental differences divide them. Unless we can begin to appreciate both the commonality and the differences, there is little hope of developing successful relations with the Soviets and their allies. In this sense citizen diplomats have broken through the either/or dichotomy of positivism to embrace the both–and polarity of human complexity. Rather than splitting the opposites, they are holding them together in creative tension. This has allowed them to appreciate in a new way the differences that have divided the two nations.

A major difference in Soviet and American societies is described by the anthropologist Edward Hall, who divides cultures into high-context and low-context types. Americans are a very low-context society. What is actually said is far more important than the larger context in which the message is sent and received. Americans emphasize specificity of content, and because they are relatively unconcerned about context, they value the qualities of flexibility and initiative. When confronted by a complex problem, Americans tend to break it down into its component parts.

The Soviets, on the other hand, have a very high-context culture. For them, the setting in which a message is sent and received is as important as the message itself. If Americans stress content, Soviets stress context. If Americans seek to break down complex problems, Soviets tend to emphasize the general setting out of which complex problems emerge. It is nearly impossible to talk about a contemporary political issue with a Soviet official without the official at some point mentioning heavy Soviet losses during the Second World War. Soviets go for the big picture. They emphasize the general over the particular, the sweep of history over immediate political concerns. Soviets know how to wait, something foreign to Americans whose entire economy is predicated on taking the waiting out of wanting.

The psychologist, Steven Kull, offers the images of a motorboat and a sailboat to explore the differences between how Americans and Soviets view themselves. Americans are like motorboats; they are inwardly motivated and emphasize their uniqueness and individuality. Americans assume that they are acting in an autonomous, inner-directed way, independent of external forces. They therefore tend to emphasize personal initiative and creativity over conformity and co-operation. For Americans, truth is an absolute perspective that they arrive at individually. They value one-to-one loyalties above those of the group. For Americans, the bigger the entity, the less their allegiance to it.

Soviets, on the other hand, are more like sailboats. Their system is such that, rather than being inner-directed, they are compelled to be more aware of the environment; metaphorically the wind, the waves and movements of the sea. They stress the situation they are in as the causal factor in their behaviour. For them, truth is derived more from social consensus than from an inner process; group loyalty is pre-eminent, especially when dealing with foreigners. The major exceptions to this are the Soviet dissidents who personify the age-old Russian tradition of courageous individuality in in the face of centralized control; exceptions that prove the rule.

Europeans lie somewhere between the Soviets and the Americans. The Soviet Union is geographically partly in Europe and shares a long history with Europe. Its political ideology was originally formulated in Europe by Europeans. One of the most fundamental similarities the Soviets share with Europeans is the notion of governance by principle, something quite foreign to Americans whose political economy is based on the absence of a cohesive principle, thus maximizing individual freedom.

It is interesting to note that Napoleon remarked, on his way back to France from his historic defeat by the Russian army in 1814, that should Germany ever be defeated or divided, Russia would take over eastern Europe. This happened in 1945, allowing the Soviets to play an integral part in European history generally, and in east European politics and culture predominantly.

The United States, on the other hand, is separated geographically from Europe by the Atlantic Ocean. It was colonized by Britain and France. It was populated primarily by disenchanted Europeans who made the decision to sever their ties with the 'old world' and create a 'new world' of their own. The US had barely overthrown the British crown by Napoleon's time. Had Napoleon reflected globally, he might have concluded that with Germany's division, America would fill the vacuum in the west just as Russia would do in the east in Europe.

Today the two superpowers hold hostage between them that continent which was the mother of them both. The 'empires' are against Europe. And yet, like the Soviets, Europeans know and appreciate governance by principle. Like Americans, Europeans appreciate governance by representative democracy. Europeans are both high- and low-context, moving sometimes more like sailboats, sometimes more like motorboats. They are therefore able both to empathize and to act as catalysts between the super-powers. However, this can only happen if Europeans take the high road towards a pan-European identity independent of the USA and USSR. Europe must liberate itself from the 'empires'. The alternative is to remain divided and to be a future battleground.

These statements are, of course, approximations. No culture is exclusively high- or low-context, nor is the European connection so clear-cut. Yet for American citizen diplomats working with Europeans and Soviets, the observations of Hall and Kull have proved useful. Basically, they carry a perspective that brings the various cultures together as being equal even though different. Citizen diplomats have become part of a larger whole, giving political meaning to the insight made by the psychologist Fritz Perls that 'contact is the appreciation of differences'.

Green Politics

In Europe, other kinds of diplomats have emerged: the Greens, who have not only directly challenged government policies but who have actually run for government office. They share many of the ideals of the citizen diplomats, a fact made clear by the statement that 'We are neither left nor right. We are in front'. While citizen diplomats have taken responsibility for international relations, the Greens have felt personal responsibility for issues that range across the political spectrum, from international affairs to the environment, from government relations to individual spirituality. What they share with the citizen diplomats is a similar commitment to finding a new appropriate way of life in the midst of ancient antagonisms.

For the Greens, nuclear weapons are a symptom of a crisis that is global, multi-faceted and inter-related. It presents the whole human race with a very dangerous opportunity. Billions of dollars are spent on arms while millions starve, most of them children. Most of our rivers are polluted. Much of our land is poisoned. Our urban air has become unfit to breathe. Human relations are weighed down by competition and alienation. The international arena is full of bullies, terrorists and thieves.

One cannot 'fix' the prevailing world system, the Greens argue, one can only overcome the present crisis by developing an entirely new paradigm – a new type of diplomacy as different from traditional diplomacy as Einstein's physics is from Newton's. In the face of environmental exploitation, the Greens work for ecological sensitivity; in the face of division and enmity, for wholeness and neighbourliness. The Greens emphasize the interconnectedness and interdependence of not only all humans, but of humanity with the earth herself, rejecting thereby all forms of exploitation and violence whether they be personal, social or national.

From the perspective of our current crisis, all this sounds utopian, even more utopian than the notion that individual citizens, working independently of government, can and should play an active role in international relations. But it is perhaps precisely because of this quality that the Greens have been so successful, particularly in West Germany and Sweden. They have been so refreshingly different, so idealistic, that despite the rigidities of European political structures and their own internal divisions, they have sparked a movement that is now worldwide. As one of their slogans puts it, 'If you don't have a dream, you have no power to fight'.

Notwithstanding the fact that several of the basic principles of the Greens – nonviolence, ecological concern and grassroots democracy – were inspired by the American civil rights and environmental movements, they are very European in style and specifically German in origin. In a penetrating book about them called *Green Politics*, Fritjof Capra and Charlene Spretnak argue that 'their roots, their context and their memories lie on this side of the great trauma that severed the continuity of the German experience: the Nazi era'.[3]

Like most citizen diplomats, the majority of Greens were born after the Second World War. But they have reacted to their elders' support of Hitler, while their American counterparts have reacted to their elders' obsession with nuclear weapons and, therefore, communism. It is perhaps because of this difference that the Greens have been more comprehensive in their scope and concerns, while citizen diplomats have limited their activities essentially to developing relationships with the other nation with a nuclear obsession: the Soviet Union.

The forerunners of the Greens were the 'angry young Germans' of the 1960s. They, like student activists elsewhere, felt betrayed by their parents and inspired to revolt. Student protests in Germany were as common as in the United States. Yet while their American counterparts were mobilizing around the war in Vietnam, feminism and the counterculture, the German students were largely inspired by a Marxist critique of German post-war capitalism. As Capra and Spretnak put it, 'Marxism was practically the only game in town'. Although most have moved far beyond it today, Marxism was in some ways the initiation rite of most Greens under forty, with the exception of one of their principal leaders, Petra Kelly, who spent the 1960s in the United States.

During the 1960s, the young German radicals formed urban communities in which private property, monogamy and privacy were eschewed. Some participated in what one of their leaders, Rudi Dutschke, called 'the march through institutions', attempting to change society's institutions from within. Others went underground and formed groups like Baader–Meinhof, surfacing in the 1970s in flashes of violence against the state. Still others dropped out to become apolitical or to focus on inner growth.

In 1974 another even larger movement began, this one primarily concerned with protecting the environment and opposing nuclear power and its proliferation. Unlike the Marxist-oriented student radicals, those attracted to environmental issues were generally either apolitical or politically moderate. They were much more interested in developing sources of alternative energy and other appropriate technology than in debating the subtleties of Marx. The environmentalists were at first attacked by the left as being 'individualistic' and 'utopian', but this did not greatly concern them. Hundreds of thousands demonstrated against various nuclear power plants and at Gorleben, the site of West Germany's proposed nuclear waste dumps.

By 1978, the two groups began to come together. Environmentalists saw the connections between nuclear power and economic exploitation; Marxists began to see the connections between economic concerns and ecological balance; and both groups realized nuclear weapons meant the annihilation of both environment and economy. After extensive discussion, at a nationwide convention near Frankfurt in March 1979, the Green Party was formed. Two major resolutions were passed: the first involved support for a nuclear-free Europe and was largely focused on the European Economic Community's investments in nuclear power plants; the second envisioned a decentralized 'Europe of the Regions', which focused attention on the demand to dissolve both NATO and WTO.

Over the next few years the Greens developed a comprehensive political platform and organized for the national elections held in March 1983. While traditional politicians ran television ads and gave slick speeches, the Greens' most popular organizing tool was the 'Green Caterpillar', a bus that brought various German rock and New Wave musicians, as well as Green candidates, to different cities and towns for benefit concerts and brief speeches. The results of the election stunned the West Germans: although Helmut Kohl and the Christian Democrats won, the Greens captured 5.6 per cent of the vote, gaining the right to send representatives to the Bundestag.

When the Green parliamentarians walked into the Bundestag, they brought with them a new political agenda. As their Federal Programme put it:

> The Establishment parties in Bonn behave as if an infinite increase in industrial production were possible on the finite planet Earth. According to their own statements, they are leading us to a hopeless choice between the nuclear state or nuclear war, between Harrisburg or Hiroshima. The worldwide ecological crisis worsens from day to day: natural resources become more scarce; chemical waste dumps are subjects of scandal after scandal; whole species of animals are exterminated; entire varieties of plants become extinct; rivers and oceans change slowly into sewers; and humans verge on spiritual and intellectual decay in the midst of a mature, industrial, consumer society. It is a dismal inheritance we are imposing on future generations . . .
>
> We represent a total concept, as opposed to the one-dimensional, still-more-production brand of politics. Our policies are guided by long-term visions for the future and are founded on four basic principles: ecology, social responsibility, grassroots democracy, and nonviolence.[4]

Capra and Spretnak point out that the four basic principles of the Greens are based on the notion of 'deep ecology', a concept that has informed most American political activism in recent years. Deep ecology goes much deeper than the concern for environmental protection. It encompasses the study of nature's subtle web of interconnected processes, of which humanity is an integral part. This basic premise, that all of life is an interrelated and interdependent whole that cannot be cut asunder save through violence, is the fountain head from which the Green positions on politics, the economy, education, health care, culture, science and international relations spring.

The Greens work for soft energy alternatives, plans based on the energy released from the cycles of the sun, wind and water. They call for regenerative agriculture that replenishes the soil and incorporates natural means of pest control. They demand a cessation of environmental pollution and nuclear proliferation and the beginning of extensive environmental protection programmes. Viewing the world in terms of integrating systems and overlapping relationships, the Greens have also developed the concept of 'social ecology' which embraces concern for the poor and the working class in terms of equal standing with industrial productivity. It also implies a transformation of power and decision-making from a few leaders at the top to a broad-based democratic process in which local groups participate.

This notion of power requires a rejection of the structural violence that permeates so much of our society. The Greens call for peace education in the schools – teaching that trains children in the art of arbitration and compromise and shows that the cult of the soldier is a cultural phenomenon not a natural one. Calling for the end to violence and oppression against women, children and minorities, the Greens are developing schemes for non-exploitative economic systems in which the current corporate structure is replaced by employee-owned operations. As Petra Kelly puts it: 'Nonviolence is the essential ingredient in an ecological society.'

This is not to say that the Greens are unaware of the contradiction between the principles of deep ecology and the realities of twentieth-century Germany. Another leader, Roland Vogt, says quite clearly that

What we have not yet accomplished is to say how we show ourselves to be nonviolent at the moment when we participate in governmental functions, because the state is itself an institution of violence. For example, how will a Green city council act against people who don't pay their rent, although they really could because they receive welfare or because they earn enough? The normal course is warning, warning, eviction notice, and then eviction by force and by police. We haven't solved this. That is, there are still no thought-out concepts of how one can reconcile the demands of social responsibility with the demands of nonviolence.[5]

Nevertheless, one of the Greens' slogans comes from Gandhi: 'There is no way to peace; peace is the way.'

Even as the diplomacy of American citizen diplomats derives from the fact that they live in one of the superpowers, so the diplomacy of the Greens comes from their living between the superpowers. The politics of the Greens springs from their experience of living in the prime thermonuclear battlefield: West Germany is roughly the size of Oregon, although instead of having 2.5 million residents, it has 60 million, plus 5,000 American nuclear weapons and armed forces from the United States, Britain, France, Canada, Belgium, the Netherlands and Denmark. Soviet nuclear weapons are targeted on West Germany as are those of the French, and probably also those of the British. The American weapons on West German soil are of various yields and ranges. Some travel only 30 miles, which means they would be shot from West Germany and land in West Germany, presumably to 'save' West Germany from the Soviets.

Given this stark vulnerability, it is not surprising that the Greens reject categorically the relatively sanguine approach to nuclear weapons adopted by many American citizen diplomat groups. They largely refrain from publicly criticizing US (or Soviet) nuclear policies and instead emphasize the positive aspects of exchanges. The Greens maintain that the division of Europe by the two superpowers has remilitarized West Germany and resulted in the loss of real independence by the allies of the US and USSR. One of the Greens' first parliamentarians, Gert Bastian, in a book entitled *Create Peace,* calls on West Germany to ban nuclear weapons, reduce the number of foreign troops on its soil, withdraw from NATO, establish itself as a neutral state and defend its borders only with defensively equipped troops. Bastian believes that in time West Germany could become entirely weapons-free, protected only by a 'social defence' which entails large-scale public protest, economic boycotts, strikes, stalling, obstructing and non-compliance, reminiscent of Dutch, Norwegian and Danish resistance to the Nazis during the Second World War.

Because of the Marxist element in the Green Party, the Greens find it easier to criticize American foreign policy than that of the Soviet Union. They nevertheless continue to call for the dissolution of both NATO and WTO and for the withdrawal of all nuclear weapons from Europe. At the same time, they do not join most other West German groups in calling for the reunification of Germany. The Greens believe nationalism is as great an evil as militarism.

Implementation of these policies is a tall order and the Greens are not only far from succeeding but, like almost every opposition group, they have been racked by internal dissent. The Marxist elements have made an even-handed critique of both superpowers difficult and their style has alienated the prevailing majority of Germans concerned more with law and order than innovation and protest. As a result, popular support for the Greens has remained under 10 per cent. In the 1988 elections in Sweden they polled 5.6 per cent. Nevertheless, they have made their presence felt, and in the process they have inspired the formation of similar groups throughout western Europe and the United States.

Paradoxically, the weakness of the Greens is the very basis of their strength. As one of their slogans puts it: 'Demand the impossible, obtain the possible.' As Bastian explains it, this means 'We know very well that the sort of thinking necessary for our solutions hardly exists now among the population, yet it is necessary to begin to change the consciousness.'[6] This is by no means a new sentiment. It was expressed long ago by Tertullian (160-230 AD) in his aphorism *'credo quia impossibile est'* – 'I believe because it is impossible'. From this perspective, the Greens have succeeded. Along with the peace movement elsewhere, they have managed to break the post-war consensus in Europe which from 1945 to 1980 essentially accepted without question the need for a nuclear shield against the Soviets and the indispensable importance of NATO. Now opposition parties in almost every country question, if not oppose, these assumptions. While the Greens may take a long time to be a majority party, they deserve credit for breaking open the political discussion about nuclear weapons, superpower dominance and the very survival of planet earth.

Solidarity

If the Greens, in conjunction with the wider peace movement, have broken the post-war assumptions about NATO and its reliance on nuclear weapons, the Solidarity movement in Poland has made a similar breakthrough in the Warsaw Treaty Organization (WTO). In its own way, Solidarity has contributed to the greening of eastern Europe.

While citizen diplomacy and the Green movement in the west have arisen within the context of political pluralism, Solidarity took shape within the confines of totalitarianism. The prevailing wisdom in Poland until 1980, as in the rest of Europe, was that the despotic nature of the Polish regime and its Soviet military support made any effective opposition impossible.

In an article in the *New Yorker*, Jonathan Schell has drawn together many of the aspects of Solidarity that make its diplomacy so innovative and visionary.[7] Schell points out that up until the late 1970s in Poland those who worked for change fell into two camps. One, the revisionists, who sought to soften the totalitarian excesses of the Party by appealing to the humanitarian aspects of Marxist-Leninist theory. The other, the so-called neo-positivists, mostly Catholic liberals, who sought to moderate Party practices by co-operating with it from within the protection of the Church. These two groups worked within the existing system and offered a way for criticism, however limited, to be expressed, but in doing so legitimized the *status quo*.

By combining political realism and social idealism, a third way emerged in the late 1970s. It was clear that neither the Communist

Party nor the Soviet troops could be driven out of Poland. But what if the masses of people began to cast aside their fear and act with integrity within this limitation? What if Poles overstepped their political boundaries at home while accepting the geo-strategic realities abroad? It was Adam Michnik who, perhaps more than anyone, distilled the emerging alternative into a coherent vision. In an essay written in 1976 called 'A New Evolutionism', he called upon Poles to scrutinize the details of their local environments and to begin to act with the integrity of their own convictions. He rejected the path of the revisionists and neo-positivists who acknowledged the supremacy of the Party and worked to change or modify Party policies. For Michnik, a 'programme for evolution' had to be developed which would address itself to 'independent public opinion and not to totalitarian power. Such a programme would offer advice to the people regarding how to behave, not to the government regarding how to reform itself.'[8]

For people in eastern Europe this was a revolutionary concept. The only major attempt to modify communism among the Soviet satellite states had been made in 1968 in Czechoslovakia when Alexander Dubcek, the Party leader, began large-scale reforms. He had operated on the assumption that the Party held a monopoly of power. Michnik disagreed. He believed that even within a communist system there were other sources of power. It was the activation of these that led to the formation of Solidarity.

A significant step towards developing this 'new diplomacy' was the creation of the Workers' Defence Committee (KOR) in September 1976. KOR did not address itself to government; rather, it focused its attention on rendering concrete legal, financial and medical assistance to workers and their families who had suffered from government repression. It did this in a completely open and public manner. When the founders, Michnik among them, wrote their statement of purpose, they not only signed their names to it, but in an act without precedence among the opposition they added their addresses and telephone numbers as well.

Thereafter, the committee followed a policy of openness as much as possible as well as a policy of truthfulness. Whether the government spies were listening or not became irrelevant. The corollary of this was the policy of 'autonomy' of action. As another

KOR member, Jan Josef Lipski, put it: 'There was no question of ordering someone by command of the organization to do something he did not want to do . . . everything was done by people motivated by their own initiative and enthusiasm . . .'[9] The policy of autonomy required trust. When a decision had to be made regarding what steps to take to guard against government infiltration, KOR decided to reject suspicion as well as all the equipment and procedures that accompany such activity and 'trust everyone within the bounds of common sense'. Dissident intellectuals and workers were now joined by Catholic thinkers and supported by the Catholic hierarchy. In Krakow, Cardinal Wojtyla had emerged in the early 1970s as a strong advocate of human rights and of an independent intellectual life. In 1974, the Polish Communist Party ideologue, Andrezej Werblan, called the cardinal 'the only real ideological threat in Poland'.[10] Werblan's judgement was given dramatic affirmation in 1978 when Cardinal Wojtyla became Pope John Paul II.

The Pope's visits to Poland, in 1979 and 1983, crystallized the people's resentment against the rulers and strengthened their resolve. The moment he knelt to kiss the ground at Warsaw airport, he imbued the Poles with a new spirit. Although he never criticized the regime directly, his meaning was plain enough. 'The exclusion of Christ from the history of man is an act against man,' he told an enormous outdoor gathering in Warsaw. With that thinly veiled allusion to an atheistic government, a deafening roar of approval filled the huge city square. 'The Polish people broke the barrier of fear that day,' a Polish bishop later recalled. 'They were hurling a challenge at their Marxist rulers.'[11]

The spark that ignited Solidarity's 'self-limiting revolution', as Jacek Kuron described it, was a government decree in June 1980 that raised the price of meat. Polish workers had been learning from mistakes made in 1970 and 1976. This time workers occupied factories, particularly in the Lenin shipyard at Gdansk. Here Lech Walesa, an unemployed electrician who had been fired eight months earlier for trying to organize an independent trade union, eventually became the bargaining representative for most of the 500,000 strikers from the Baltic Sea to the coal-mining fields of Silesia.

Led by Walesa, the committee set forth a bold series of demands including the right to form free trade unions and the right to strike. This was something unheard of in a communist country. Initially the government refused even to discuss the issue. With the rebellion quickly spreading, however, it was faced with either negotiating or unleashing a massive blood bath. It chose to negotiate. Meeting across a wooden table in the shipyard's conference hall in August 1980, Walesa and his fellow strikers consistently out-manoeuvred the government team.

Meanwhile, the Lenin shipyard became the centre of an extraordinary national movement. Emblazoned with flowers, red and white Polish flags and portraits of Pope John Paul II, the plant's heavy iron gates came to symbolize that heady mixture of faith, courage and hope that sustained the workers through their defiance of a regime which heretofore had tolerated no dissent, let alone strikes. The world watched, wondering how long the Soviets would let such a demonstration of defiance continue before they sent their tanks in. But Walesa and his fellow strikers stood their ground and, like soldiers before battle, made confession and received communion from priests in the open shipyard.

Their firmness and patience won the day. The government finally gave in to virtually all their demands: the right to form free unions, the right to strike, reduced censorship, and access to the state controlled television and radio networks for the unions and the church. At the nationally televised ceremony, where strikers and government representatives alike stood side by side and sang the Polish national anthem, Walesa signed what became known as the Gdansk agreement with a giant souvenir pen bearing the likeness of John Paul II.

Workers across Poland rushed to join the new union, Solidarity. Soon Walesa and the other ex-strike leaders found themselves at the head of a labour federation of 10 million, 90% of the Polish workforce. Over 900,000 Polish communists left the Party after August 1980, reducing its strength to 2.5 million, and over a million joined Solidarity without resigning from the Party. The Party was on the verge of collapse. Stanislav Kania, who had replaced Gierek as Party leader in September 1980, did the most sensible thing under the circumstances: he adopted the workers' slogan of *odonowa* (renewal) in the hope of controlling the new union from the top and limiting its scope. At the same time he co-operated with Solidarity to avoid a possibly disastrous confrontation.

After thirty-five years of Stalinism, the challenge of bringing freedom to Poland was an awesome and complicated one. The rank and file workers of Solidarity had an insatiable drive for democracy but no practical experience about how to function as a group. Most of the Solidarity activists were young and simultaneously bitter and exuberant: bitter over the Party's economic bankruptcy and moral corruption and exuberant over their new-found strength. As time went on, more and more people who had in one way or another been crushed or maltreated by the regime used Solidarity as a forum to vent their frustration and call for a radical reformulation of not just the economy but the government itself. These currents grew stronger as the months went by and the government failed to demonstrate the moral will necessary to eradicate the causes of the crisis.

Decades of blatant propaganda, ruthless leadership and economic failures had discredited the authorities in the eyes of the public. With a Party shrunken by defections to Solidarity, the majority who were left were die-hard Stalinists and careerists who had fallen into a state of paralysis. They were unwilling to give in to the demands being made and yet were powerless to assert Party control over the restless masses. 'If the government had actually produced a golden egg,' gibed Kuron, 'people would say it was not golden; second, that it was not an egg; and third, that the government had stolen it.'

What erupted across Poland was a diversity of civic activity of unprecedented proportions. In the process, Poles, split apart and alienated by over forty years of totalitarianism, now reunited in a way that radicalized the meaning of revolution. The classic formula, enunciated most clearly by Lenin, was to seize state power first and then embark on social change. Solidarity reversed this order. It began to embark on the business of social change and only then turned its attention to the state. 'Its principle,' as Schell puts it, 'was to start doing the things you think should be done, and to start being what you think society should become.' Quite simply, Solidarity acted as if Polish people were already free while remaining perfectly clear that Poland was not. By keeping their actions small, limited, non-threatening, Poles discovered liberty. In discovering liberty, they discovered strength.

This came as a complete surprise to both Solidarity and the government. In 1970, protesting workers had attempted to demonstrate power in the face of the state. They were brutalized by police, whereupon they marched to some nearby government buildings and burned them down. The repression afterwards was as bad as before. Learning from this, Jacek Kuron summarized the new mandate: 'Don't burn down Committees; found your own.' In doing so, Solidarity discovered it had undreamed of power, but not that which was based in official institutions. Solidarity's power came from the people themselves.

A paradox emerged, says Schell. People at all levels of society acted at times as if there were no repressive government at all in Poland. Solidarity thus completely failed to anticipate the government's response: the imposition of martial law. At the same time the government misjudged the power of the people and was taken off-guard at the crucial negotiations in Gdansk in August 1980. The two sides misjudged one another because one was manipulating power and the other did not yet know its own strength. To the government, the opposition seemed impotent because it lacked weapons and a discernible hierarchy or institutional base. To Solidarity the government seemed weak because it had no popular support. The idealism of Solidarity made the imposition of martial law an impossibility for them; the realism of the government made even the existence of Solidarity a matter of incredulity.

In his *Warsaw Diary*, Ryszard Kapuscinski writes:

> Here everything is based on a certain principle of asymmetrical verification: the system promises to prove itself *later* concerning a general happiness that exists only in the future, but demands that you prove yourself now, *today*, by demonstrating your loyalty, consent, and diligence. You commit yourself to everything; the system to nothing.[12]

'The opposition,' Schell explains, 'worked in exactly the opposite way. It proved itself *today*, and let *later* take care of itself.' In the process, Solidarity evolved a new approach to one of the most insoluble problems of confronting both ethics and politics – the question of ends and means.

There has always been in society a discrepancy between noble goals and ignoble means, between the necessity for deceit in political arenas where manipulation and force rule supreme, and the grand intentions of the visionaries towards which these means are directed. Does the end justify the means? Or is the nature of the process as important as the goal?

Schell makes the important observation that in Poland ends and means became synonymous. Every end became a means, every means an end. Each of the means of KOR – openness, truthfulness, autonomy, trust – was also an end. In the face of totalitarianism, each honest and public act became a goal in and of itself, an act of defiance in the face of government deceit. The intent to change the government was relinquished; only the integrity of the individual in the spontaneity of the moment mattered. For the government evil means for good ends were the norm. For Solidarity good means were essential for good ends.

It is within this context that Schell makes an interesting point about nonviolence. Any use of violence, he says, would have spoiled the wellspring of both Solidarity's strength and virtue. Its directness of approach, its local emphasis, its rejection of deceit formed a self-consistent whole. And yet to call this nonviolence seems almost too weak, too restrictive, because along with being nonviolent Solidarity was non-secretive, non-coercive and non-deceptive. And it was so by design. These principles were the results of the positive vision of life – a pursuit of an open and honest society energized by the integrity of free individuals. This meant its strength would have been decimated had it resorted to violence. Schell sums it up: 'A little violence would probably have been as harmful to Solidarity as a little pacifism would be to an army in the middle of a war.'

In modern times, Schell observes, the introduction of spiritual or moral values into the nitty-gritty of politics has been regarded with suspicion, to say the least. Public response to citizen diplomats and the Greens are good examples of this. The City of God and the City of Man do not join walls in peoples' minds; they exist in separate spheres. The City of God cannot associate with mundane means because its purity, upon which its authority is based, would be ruined. The City of Man cannot adopt purity in its means because it will not be able to conquer the wicked. Any attempt to join evil means to good ends only serves to give licence to the fanatics.

Yet keeping the two Cities separate runs a similar risk. The ethical principles of religion lose their power if it is acknowledged that there is a realm of society where they do not or cannot apply. At the same time, political life without a moral referent can rest on no other value than the raw exercise of power, and this means a social life of barbarism.

Down through the ages, people have tried various ways of combining the two, from Plato's notion of the philosopher king to Machiavelli's articulation of one morality for politics, another for the private individual. Solidarity, like the citizen diplomats and the Greens, eased the tension between the moral and the political by adopting a method of action that did not differentiate means from ends. This allowed the spiritual and moral energies of Poles to flow into the political world largely uncorrupted, at least for a brief moment in time. With Solidarity, the two Cities came to rest on one foundation: respect for the dignity and worth of each individual. That is why Solidarity still survives.

As the Polish government's imposition of martial law in December 1981 demonstrates, this vision does not lead to the Promised Land. But it did succeed in creating a space where citizens in the public realm behaved by the same standards they used for private acts. Living by this principle means, of course, that political life will be no closer to perfection than private life. Yet it also means that politics can no longer be singled out as an area where certain evils not tolerated in private life could be publicly condoned.

In its own way, therefore, Solidarity offers a way to humanize the conflict between governments and peoples. By accepting the fragilities of the individual, it has come to terms with the realities of the nation. Solidarity acknowledges that Soviet control cannot be removed from Poland in the foreseeable future and that Poles must accommodate to this fact in one way or another. The acceptance of this reality, without subjugating the mind to it, would lead to the acknowledgement of the paradox that good and evil are distributed just about equally everywhere. One can only hope, as Solidarity has, along with the Greens and the citizen diplomats, that in this perennial struggle the good has the chance to advance a little.

Epilogue

NUÑEZ THE Conquistador was confronted with either death or healing. We face the same stark choice. Some of us have become numbed to the idea of the cold war and potential death; others are learning to heal, which first entails finding integration in themselves. The ability to transcend one's own sense of separateness and become more aware of the essential unity of life is a recurrent theme in the literature, mythology and folklore of all cultures at all times. It is both historically specific and a timeless and universal human phenomenon.

The good we have discussed here is not an abstraction. It is an historical imperative, conditioned by an infection of historical time called enmity. Diplomacy, in the tradition of Machiavelli, has become a legitimation of enmity, a manipulation of means to accomplish the goals of power, greed and exploitation. At the hands of the new diplomats, diplomacy has become an art form, an instrument to implement certain ideals within the limitations of mundane politics.

The new diplomats must not be given too much credit, nor should the traditional diplomats be subjected to derision or scorn. In the end, history amply demonstrates that people get pretty much what they deserve. There is a strange symbiosis between the leader and the led, between private prejudice and public conduct. Looking back, Hitlers and Stalins represented their times as much as Gandhis and Martin Luther Kings.

There is no question that our century has been one of unparalleled violence and unsurpassed exploitation. Two world wars left 80 million dead. Over a hundred armed conflicts since 1945 have cost over a hundred million lives. Enmity has had many faces, our fears many corners in our hearts to hide.

At the same time, our century has exploded with social and technological progress. We have seen the start of the liberation of women, the repudiation at official levels of racism (except in South Africa) and the concerted attempt to end hunger and a multitude of diseases. Computers and other aspects of high technology have put people on the moon, explored the inner recesses of molecular life, created the possibility of new organ transplants in the human body. Ours has been a century of extreme opposites. We have experienced colonialism and national liberation and the split of the world into two hostile camps, reminiscent of ancient Athens and Sparta. Between them lie the non-aligned nations – both a battleground and a source of natural wealth for the two superpowers.

Our religious and philosophical traditions have taught us to split the opposites, to war against that which is not us. We have been divided between the elect and the damned, between the logical and the illogical, between the provable and the subjective. We are products of a tradition that has taught us to subjugate that which we exclude. From the Jews conquering the inhabitants of Canaan, to the Christians condemning the heathen to hell, to the European imperialists colonizing virtually the rest of the planet, we have divided and conquered, empowered by the philosophical tradition that has separated the logic of our intellect from the sensibilities of our soul.

All this concrete, and yet the flowers bloom. In the final analysis, life wants to live. What this means, in an age in which the logic of enmity is annihilation, is that there must be an intuitive reconnection of the opposites. Complementarity must replace exclusivity; awareness of the inner relatedness between things formerly thought separate must reimpose itself upon the current disconnection of things which in their essence are one.

Both the disconnections and the internal relatedness are equally real in our world. Soviets and Americans are genuinely different, but they are also fundamentally the same, even as men and women are obviously distinct beings but share a common humanity: separate but equal, separate because we are different, equal because we are the same.

Citizen diplomats and traditional diplomats, Greens and NATO officials, Solidarity and the Polish government – each have roles to play in a very complex world in which good and evil, capitalism and communism, weapons and hope co-exist, perhaps not in equal measures, but certainly with equal validity.

Our task is to discern the appropriateness of each, to know when to leave the one and begin the other and how to combine with sophistication the subtleties of each. It is the interplay of light and dark that produces the spectrum of colours that makes up the rainbow.

It is in this spirit that we must look at those whom we have been taught to call enemies and see the things we have projected upon them because we lack the courage to confront those qualities in ourselves. We must understand that our weapons of total destruction have arisen from a desperate urge for limitless power. We have to learn submission to the wisdom of limits.

Finally, we must learn to become as eternally vigilant about the needs for human survival as we have become in the preservation of our political freedoms. Like it or not, ours is the first generation to have called human survival into question. This is our legacy, a choice that, like liberty, from our generation forward will have to be examined and chosen again and again. It has been our curse to invent nuclear weapons. It is now our challenge to prove that human life is more invincible than those weapons. In order to succeed in this, we have to embark on the journey beyond enmity.

Notes

1 The cold war and the insight gap

1 D. Rowe, *Living with the Bomb*, 1985: 35.
2 J.R. Macy, *Despair and Personal Power in the Nuclear Age*, 1983: 12–14.

2 Absolute weapons, absolute enemies

1 NSC-68 was declassified in 1975. See T.H. Etzold and J. Lewis (eds) *Containment: Documents on American Policy and Strategy, 1945-1950*, New York, Columbia University Press, 1978: 385-442.
2 Dean Acheson, *Present at Creation*, New York, Norton, 1969: 374.
3 *Common Sense and the Present Danger*, Committee on the Present Danger Publication: 2.
4 Fred M. Kaplan, 'The Soviet Civil Defense Myth', *Bulletin of the Atomic Scientists*, April 1978: 42.
5 See Horst Richter, address given to 2nd Congress of International Physicians for the Prevention of Nuclear War, Cambridge, England, 1982.
6 Ibid.
7 T. Merton, *Red or Dead: the Anatomy of a Cliché.* 1965.
8 Richter, address, op.cit.

3 Enemy images

1 J.D. Frank, 'Breaking the thought barrier', *Psychiatry*, 23, 1960: 250-66.
2 Ibid.
3 H. Cantrill, 'Perception and interpersonal relations', *American Journal of Psychiatry*, II, 1957, 114: 119-26.
4 L.J. Halle, 'The struggle called coexistence', *New York Times* magazine, 15 Nov. 1959: 110.
5 Frank, 'Breaking the thought barrier': 250-66.
6 Ibid.
7 *Baltimore Sunday Sun*, 8 Nov. 1959.
8 H.A. Wilmer, 'Towards a definition of the therapeutic community', *American Journal of Psychiatry*, 1958, 114: 824-34.
9 See D. Campbell, 'What really happened to KE 007', *New Statesman*, 26 April 1985: 8-10.

10 J.E. Mack, 'The perception of US-Soviet intentions and other psychological dimensions of the nuclear arms race', *American Journal of Orthopsychiatry,* 52(4), October 1982.
11 C. Pinderhughes, 'Differential bonding: towards a psycho-physiological theory of stereotyping', *American Journal of Psychiatry,* 1979, 136.
12 J.D. Frank, *Sanity and Survival,* 1968: 104.

4 Mirror images

1 U. Bronfenbrenner, 'The mirror image in Soviet-American relations: A Social Psychologist's Report', *Journal of Social Issues,* 17(3), 1961: 45–56.
2 Ibid: 48.
3 Ibid.
4 Ibid: 51.
5 Ibid: 52.
6 S. Oskamp, 'Attitudes towards US and Russian actions: a double standard', *Psychological Reports,* 1965, 16: 43–6.
7 J.D. Frank, *Sanity and Survival.*
8 *The Times,* 3 January 1985.
9 A. Horne, *New York Times,* 20 February 1966.
10 J.D. Frank, *Sanity and Survival:* 116–17.
11 Berriman, *the Bulletin of Atomic Scientists,* 1964.
12. *Detente,* April 1985.

5 Groupthink

1 F. Heller, 'The dangers of groupthink', *Guardian,* 31 January 1983.
2 J. Thompson, *Psychological Aspects of Nuclear War,* 1985: 85.
3 D.R. Holsti, 1972, quoted in J. Thompson, *Psychological Aspects of Nuclear War.*

6 The fortress of postitivism

1 J.B. Priestley, *Man and Time,* 1964: 150.
2 D. Bakan, 'The interface between war and the social sciences', *American Psychological Association,* Los Angeles, 1981.
3 J. Schell, *The Fate of the Earth,* 1982: 138–39.

7 'Specializing' the truth

1   L. Peattie, *Bulletin of the Atomic Scientists*, June 1984.
2   R.J. Lifton, 'Beyond psychic numbing: a call to awareness', *American Journal of Orthopsychiatry*, 1982, 52: 618-29.
3   V.E. Frankl, *Man's Search for Meaning:* 79-80.
4   In Peattie, *Bulletin of the Atomic Scientists*.
5   Ibid.
6   Ibid.
7   Milgram, *Obedience to Authority*, 1974.

8   Changing perceptions

1   P. Bateson, 'Cooperation', university sermon, King's College, Cambridge, 19 May 1985.
2   Ibid.
3   J.R. Durant, 'The beast in man: an historical perspective on the biology of human aggression', in P.F. Brian and D. Benton (eds), *The Biology of Aggression*, 1981: 17-46.
4   Ibid.
5   Ibid.
6   Ibid.
7   H. Long, *The Marvellous Adventure of Cabeza de Vaca*, 1975.

9   The new diplomats

1   This section is based on an essay written by James Garrison and James Hickman, 'The psychological principles of citizen diplomacy', in *Private Diplomacy with the Soviet Union*, Georgetown University and American Universities Publishers, 1986.
2   W.D. Davidson and J.V. Montville, 'Foreign policy according to Freud', *Foreign Policy*, 45, Winter, 1981-2.
3   Capra and Spretnak in collaboration with Rüdiger Lutz, *Green Politics: The Global Promise*, 1985: 11.
4   Ibid: 30.
5   Ibid: 43.
6   Ibid: 75.
7   *New Yorker*, 3 February 1986: 47-67.
8   Ibid: 52.
9   Ibid: 58.
10 Ibid: 59.
11 Ibid: 61.
12 Ibid: 64.